Praise for *Radical Inclusion*

"In *Radical Inclusion*, General Martin Dempsey and Ori Brafman offer current and aspiring leaders extraordinary insights into getting the best possible information for decision making as well as how to rely on trust and participation to forge strong teams. At a time when technology and, too often, organizational structures promote separateness and division, Dempsey and Brafman, through extensive use of both moving and amusing anecdotes, highlight the importance for all leaders of listening, inclusiveness, and respect as critical leadership tools for bringing unity of effort and success. These tools work, and watching General Dempsey apply them to great effect in multiple command positions led me to recommend him to the president to be Chairman of the Joint Chiefs of Staff. There is great advice in these pages, based on real-world experience."
—ROBERT M. GATES, U.S. Secretary of Defense, 2006–2011

"*Radical Inclusion* is an indispensable read for anyone in a leadership position today. Dempsey and Brafman, an unlikely duo, eloquently examine critical principles of leadership in our current digital world and provide a foundation to change top-down hierarchy and evolve with the times. A compelling and very important book."
—PATTY McCORD, former chief talent officer, Netflix,
and author of *Powerful*

"True leadership has never been more important for the world than it is today, yet the way we think about leadership hasn't kept pace with the changing nature of our time. We are all part of a global community, and this requires stewardship for the world as a whole—being responsive and responsible, being integrative and inclusive. And this is what makes *Radical Inclusion* so timely and relevant. Dempsey and Brafman have thoughtfully identified emerging leadership principles which demand serious consideration. They challenge us to revitalize our thinking about leadership by providing new insights and concrete tools about how we listen, amplify, and include. A refreshing read!"
—KLAUS SCHWAB, founder and executive chairman,
World Economic Forum

"Building a team—whether in sports, in the military, in business, or in foreign policy—takes leadership with heart, with dedication, and with trust. *Radical Inclusion* should be on the nightstand of anyone who aspires to lead."

    —MIKE KRZYZEWSKI, head coach, Duke University men's basketball

"Dempsey and Brafman's book offers great insight into the central paradox of power: the more we try to bolster our power by increasing control, the less actual power we will have and the less effective will our leadership be. It is such a timely message for an age in desperate need of effective leaders who, in a spirit of radical inclusion, build bridges rather than walls."

    —FR. JOHN I. JENKINS, president, University of Notre Dame

"Cutthroat balkanization in our culture and politics. The demise of agreed-upon facts as the basis for argument. The cultivation of grievance to divide and radicalize and exploit. If you are enervated or despairing of these worsening twenty-first-century dynamics, read *Radical Inclusion*. General Dempsey and Professor Brafman have mapped a way out that is practical, fascinatingly counterintuitive, and yes—radical. *Radical Inclusion* is the first thing I've read that feels like a light in the darkness for America in 2018 and beyond."

    —RACHEL MADDOW, host, *The Rachel Maddow Show*, MSNBC

"In their book, Ori Brafman and Martin Dempsey lay out a compelling vision for leadership in an increasingly uncertain world. Borrowing from unlikely sources such as Burning Man and the maker/tech world, they make the case for how upside-down models of command and control based on inclusion and collaboration are vital for our military to be successful, and indeed for any organization or business. It's essential reading for leaders of all stripes."

    —MATTHEW STEPKA, venture investor and former vice president, Google

"In *Radical Inclusion*, General Martin Dempsey and Ori Brafman have written a playbook for leadership in the twenty-first century. Concise and compelling, it lays out practical principles that will help leaders at every level and in every sector navigate the challenges of a digital and polarized world. I've had the good fortune of working closely with General Dempsey and I highly recommend this book."

    —ADAM SILVER, commissioner, National Basketball Association

RADICAL
INCLUSION

What the Post-9/11 World Should
Have Taught Us About Leadership

MARTIN DEMPSEY

and

ORI BRAFMAN

Missionday

Published in 2018 by Missionday
Printed in the United States of America
Distributed by Publishers Group West
Interior design by Tabitha Lahr

ISBN (hardcover): 978-1-939714-10-7
ISBN: (ebook): 978-1-939714-12-1
Library of Congress Control Number: 2017918362

To contact the publisher, go to: inquiries@missionday.com.

10 9 8 7 6 5 4 3 2 1

DEDICATION

MARTIN DEMPSEY: I dedicate this book to those who showed me the real meaning of leadership. My grandparents, who had the courage to leave their home in Ireland with the simple hope of making a better life in the land of opportunity that is America. My parents, who sacrificed absolutely everything for their five children. My wife and lifelong partner, Deanie, who has always been the real leader in the Dempsey family. My three children—Chris, Megan, and Caity—who encouraged me to pursue a career of service and who then joined me in that life. My protégés, who were in a very special way also my mentors. I've been blessed to learn from the best and now hope to share the knowledge with you.

ORI BRAFMAN: I dedicate this book to my parents, Tsilla and Hagay, and my brother Rom—all of whom have shown me unwavering acceptance throughout my life—and to all those who have taught me important lessons about inclusion, from the deserts of El Paso to Black Rock City and from the halls of UC Berkeley's Peace and Conflict Studies department to the tiny office of Vegan Action.

CONTENTS

PART 4: IN INCLUSION WE TRUST

PREFACE

Often the best things result from the most unexpected collaborations. Based on this belief—a belief at the very core of this book—we set out to examine today's leadership environment and to share some insights about how to navigate it. We concluded that a forty-one-year-old UC Berkeley professor and a forty-one-year-veteran U.S. Army general have very little in common except a deep and unwavering belief that most of the hard problems we face in our businesses, in our local communities, at the national level, and internationally can be solved with better leadership. Along the way, we learned that listening to each other was the first and most important step in our journey and that including diverse perspectives always produced surprising and valuable leadership insights. Ultimately we arrived at a message and how we would deliver it, a task that felt both more difficult and more important with the passage of time.

We feel a genuine urgency about our message. Few would dispute our assertion that the world began to change dramatically in 2001, but we have found the character and pace of change since 2001 more remarkable than we expected: challenges to the predictable and familiar "order of things" in business, government, international relations, and even our sense of national identity; increasing religious extremism; the emergence of global peer competitors; the proliferation of technology, and—since about 2010—ubiquitous access to data and information for virtually everybody, all the time, everywhere. Status quo companies, militaries, countries—those that for a very long time enjoyed unchallenged power—are now palpably fearful that their power is eroding. Their instinct is to exert control. It's the wrong instinct.

• • •

Although the world has changed, the way we think about leadership hasn't kept pace. Often the result is suboptimal objectives decided upon too late, measured with the wrong metrics, and implemented with overconfidence by a workforce that is not sufficiently empowered to deliver them.

This book challenges us to refresh our thinking about leadership. It's not that the things we've always done as leaders won't work anymore. In fact, we will suggest that some of them should be reinforced. But we'll also suggest that there are several emerging leadership principles and instincts that are gaining in importance and that demand careful thought and serious consideration—that is, if we want our leadership to match the times and meet their challenges.

To be sure, this book was written during a period of considerable political disagreement about our country's future, especially about how much selectivity to exert about who belongs within and who is excluded outside our borders and our communities. But this book is not a commentary on political leadership. While we'd like to think that it has something to offer to those who have been elected to lead the country through the most pressing issues of our time, we believe that it will most strongly resonate among organizational leaders, especially those facing industry, market, and cultural transformations. This book is an exploration of what happens when there's a mutation in the very core DNA of an organization.

Whether it's being a member of a family, attending a school, or serving our country, belonging to a community or a cause bigger than ourselves is core to our very humanity in three specific ways: belonging shapes our identity, it provides our sense of security, and it creates the order we need to survive.

We develop our identity based on the communities we join ("I'm a dad," "I'm an American," "I'm a soldier"). Being part of a community, in turn, provides us with security—when a parent sacrifices everything for their kids, when a teammate stays late to help a coworker finish a project, and in a thousand other ways, being a part of a community means that there are others who are committed to our success. Finally, in being a part of a community, we can expect our fellow members to abide by a certain set of rules, making our day-to-day existence predictable and thus productive.

Part of the very contract of belonging, though, is exclusion. We cluster ourselves in neighborhoods, hold tryouts for sports teams, and require exams for certain schools, thereby creating a sense of belonging among those who make the cut. Soldiers will often do anything—even against their own interests—to help a fellow combatant. This bond is so strong that we have a name for it: brothers in arms. You are brothers because you've both gone through boot camp, you both wear the same uniform, you both fight for the same country.

But what happens when there's a simple change in a company's organizational structure, or even a country's? Rather than being selective—or having any barriers to entry at all—what happens when a community is open for *anyone* to join?

We'll begin by looking at the forces knocking down organizational fences and checkpoints. We'll explore how selectivity—

border control, if you will—comes at an economic cost that may or may not make sense.

What are the costs of control? Clearly, there's a measurable economic price to keeping a sentry at the gate. But in exerting control, we may be paying a more serious but harder-to-measure cost: the ability to accurately view reality.

Indeed, it has become a cliché to say that we live in a complex, unpredictable, and rapidly changing world—so cliché, in fact, that we fail to appreciate how profoundly people are affected by it.

In 1770 John Adams declared that "facts are stubborn things." Today, we argue, facts are vulnerable. Emerging technology is making facts increasingly vulnerable, and all of us will soon have trouble discerning what is actually true. Simply put, we're about to enter an age where facts will no longer be reliable. The information we think is 100 percent accurate may be flawed, and even our best attempt to find the truth may fall short.

In a 2004 book, Ralph Keyes used the term "post-truth" to describe an emerging period in our history where the "borders blur between truth and lies, honesty and dishonesty, fiction and nonfiction."[1]

We build on that observation and explore what the world will look like when, to gain understanding of the reality around us, there is no longer a debate of facts but rather a competition of narratives. As competing narratives vie to present a picture of the world, we will have a harder time determining what's real and accurate.

Welcome to the era of the *digital echo*, where information passes from individual to individual more quickly but in the process often becomes distorted.

We will explain the phenomenon of the digital echo in great

---

1. Ralph Keyes, *"The Post-Truth Era: Dishonesty and Deception in Contemporary Life,"* no date, https://ralphkeyes.com/book/the-post-truth-era/.

detail, but it is important to note from the start that it is a neutral force. It can inform, misinform, educate, entertain, inspire the human spirit to great acts of compassion, or unleash mankind's darkest instincts. It can inspire the generosity of the "ice bucket challenge" or the hatred of the ISIS terrorist ideology. It presents both a leadership challenge and a leadership opportunity.

One thing is clear about the digital echo: it creates the need for inclusion.

In this new world, we need to leverage inclusion to gain better information about the world around us and to effectively communicate our message.

In order to help you accomplish these two imperatives, we provide concrete leadership tools to create an environment of inclusion:

1. Belonging isn't optional: give them memories. We will argue that the first step in building a team is developing in its members a sense of belonging. Consider the alternative: if leaders don't make those who follow feel a sense of belonging, someone or something else will. And the ubiquitous presence of the digital echo makes this not only possible but likely.

2. Connect effort with meaning: make it matter. We will show that persuading members of the team that their contributions matter is crucial to team success. We all want to believe we make a difference. Leaders help their followers understand what that takes.

3. Think about what you're not thinking about: learn to imagine. We will encourage leaders to develop mindfulness, awareness, and imagination through a lifelong commitment to learning. We believe and will convince all who aspire to lead that imagination is a learned attribute.

4. Prevent decision paralysis: develop a bias for action. We will demonstrate that, when presented with a problem, leaders must look for what they can do in the moment. They must avoid information paralysis. They must act to change the environment and to learn, and then act again, in a deliberate pattern of persistent learning and proactive leadership.

5. Collaborate at every level of the organization: co-create context. We will discuss how the most effective leaders harvest knowledge and empower the organization from bottom to top. We will show the benefits of concentrating the "what" while distributing the "how."

6. Expand the circle: relinquish control to build and sustain power. We will assert in the strongest terms that finding optimal, enduring, affordable solutions to complex problems requires leaders to reconsider and rebalance their understanding of the relationship among leadership, power, and control.

The leadership instincts are *listen, amplify, include.*

Neither the principles nor the instincts are an à la carte menu. Effective leaders must understand and practice all of them.

We've titled our book *Radical Inclusion* because we believe that the traditional relationship among leadership, power, and control has changed. Solving our problems by leading with an emphasis on exclusion, jealously husbanding power, and aspiring to greater control is producing suboptimal, fragile, and costly outcomes.

The alternative is to rebalance the relationship among leadership, power, and control with an emphasis on inclusion, to selectively and purposefully relinquish control to enhance power, to define success less in terms of power and control and more in the ability to achieve optimal, enduring, and affordable outcomes.

Counterintuitive? Perhaps. But as the digital echo spreads, as complex issues multiply, as uncertainty increases, as technology exponentially changes, and as risk rises, it seems reasonable that we should seek to lead by sharing our challenges rather than owning them outright.

That said, this book's proposition about leadership is not that we ought to surrender our hard-earned power because possessing it is becoming a liability. Rather, it is that we must develop an instinct for seeking opportunities to share control in order to preserve and even enhance the power we possess.

Ours is a pragmatic proposal. We advocate sharing control in problem solving not because we wish to become somehow more egalitarian but because we want to solve problems effectively and efficiently, and we want them to stay solved!

Finally, we chose the adjective "radical" to describe the kind of inclusion we advocate because it speaks to the extremes we encounter as leaders in the world today. It is our belief that concentrations of power and exclusivity will continue to form but cannot endure in a world that sees all, a world in which technology levels all, a numbingly fast-paced world of rising expectations, glaring disparities, and declining trust.

If we're right about that, about the environment in which the affairs of business, industry, international relations, and national security must be managed, then only the leader who can harness the power inherent in inclusion will make lasting progress and achieve enduring success.

PART 1
THE OPERATING ENVIRONMENT

CHAPTER 1: **THE DIGITAL ECHO**

The Fog of War Descends on Berkeley

Berkeley police sergeant Sabrina Reich wore a clear and focused expression when we talked to her in the basement of Sproul Hall on the UC Berkeley campus.

The sergeant's voice nonetheless shifted as she told us, "In the entire history of the campus, what happened is unprecedented. We didn't expect something like *this.*"

By "unprecedented" the sergeant meant Molotov cocktails, damaged property, and masked perpetrators who were either right-wing extremists, paid agitators, or anarchists out of control. In the blink of an eye Berkeley had turned into a war zone; dozens of civilians took to the streets and engaged in full-on armed conflict.

What was most alarming was that the violence seemed to emerge out of nowhere. The police were taken so completely by surprise that they simply stood by and watched. The shockwaves from the day's events reached all the way to the White House, escalating tensions between the federal government and the State of California.

And no one saw it coming. Wednesday, February 1, 2017, started out as a glorious Bay Area day. Over the previous month, after years of severe drought, California had finally been getting the drenching it so desperately needed. This week offered a respite from the rain. As temperatures rose in the afternoon, UC Berkeley students basked in glimpses of sunshine as they lounged on the steps of Sproul Hall.

Unlike the manicured, palm-lined drives of Stanford, its archrival an hour to the south, Cal has a decidedly gritty feel to it. It's an urban campus where you're as likely to run across a drum circle as you are to be caught up in a political debate. The guy in front of you in line for coffee could be a hippie, or he could be a Nobel laureate (Cal has reserved parking spots for Nobel Prize recipients)—or he could be both.

While the tech start-ups and venture capitalists may get more attention, it's impossible to understand Silicon Valley without understanding what's happening at Berkeley.

We often think of the transformational innovation coming from San Jose, Cupertino, and Mountain View, all home to the massive tech companies. Likewise, in Menlo Park and Palo Alto venture capital funds deploy billions of dollars. But Berkeley is the epicenter of social imagination—the place where the conscience of Silicon Valley originates.

It was on the Sproul Hall steps that Mario Savio stood to lead the free speech movement, and he walked through the administration building's doors for the very first sit-ins just forty years ago. This is where protest movements from civil right to animal rights were launched.

Berkeley is no stranger to diversity of speech, and the campus is no stranger to controversial voices. At the peak of the AIDS epidemic, for instance, Professor Peter Duesberg gave a talk claiming that HIV wasn't caused by a virus but was instead the product of drugs and a party lifestyle. Protesters objected to the presentation, predicting that it would impact HIV policy—and indeed, South Africa went on to base its policies on Duesberg's theories.

For decades the campus has prided itself on being accepting of an eclectic cast of characters, from religious protesters to antinuclear activists to proud nudists. So tolerant are the campus and community of a variety of speech that local businesses sometimes sponsor protesters, paying them to display ads on the backs of their picket signs. When outspoken conservative activist Milo Yiannopoulos announced that Berkeley would be his final stop on the year-long tour he had dubbed an "all-out war on social justice," while you couldn't have expected the student body to be thrilled, you wouldn't have expected an actual war.

At one university on the tour, his appearance led to the resignation of the chancellor; at another appearance the protests grew so tense that a bystander was shot in the abdomen. Fearing similar outcomes, other universities preemptively canceled Yiannopoulos's appearances.

On the day of his appearance at Berkeley, tensions were running high. Student anxiety over Yiannopoulos's speech wasn't necessarily about the views he might express. Various campus groups worried that he might do something like call out undocumented students, as rumors to that effect had been swirling on social media—and were validated by an open letter sent to Berkeley students on February 1 by the university's Office of Student Affairs.

University officials feared violent clashes among protesters. The University of California Police Department stepped in, requiring the Berkeley College Republicans to raise $10,000 to cover the costs of security—which initially seemed to pay off, as the evening started with a peaceful protest and dance party against the rainbow-illuminated backdrop of the administration building.

Here's where things took a turn.

According to one version of events, reported by national media and believed by those in our nation's capital inclined to think the worst of Berkeley, at 5:39 p.m. student protesters began moving to block the venue entrance, and twenty-one minutes later Milo was evacuated. At 6:03 p.m. students shot fireworks at the building, and over the next ten minutes the protesters broke fences and windows. In response, police fired rubber bullets and tear gas into the crowd. Things only escalated from there, as protesters broke the windows of the student building and threw Molotov cocktails erupting in flames that lit up Sproul Plaza.

The next day the White House escalated the situation further with a thinly veiled threat: if Berkeley couldn't keep student violence from erupting over speech, perhaps the university wasn't deserving of federal funds.

Politics aside, you can see the origin of the concern: how could a campus that prides itself on tolerance condone vandalism and violent behavior by its students? Indeed, playing Monday-morning quarterback, you might think that the university should have exerted more control, hiring more police officers and vetting student groups to prevent the chaos that ensued.

But something didn't add up. When we dug a little deeper, we found that the administration, the media, and virtually everyone else following the story had gotten it completely wrong.

The problem with the students-are-to-blame version of events is that the student organizers of the protest were residents of a co-op that abided by nonviolent ideologies.

Think about that for a moment. These are students with majors like development studies and environmental science who toss around phrases like "community spirit" and "global consciousness." Sure, they might be guilty of smoking pot, but they aren't the Molotov-cocktail-throwing type.

In fact, knowing that the protests might create tensions,

the organizers actually went to great effort to underscore their nonviolent intentions. "We are not here to engage in physical confrontation," they wrote on the flyer they distributed to draw a crowd. "We will protect each other," they continued, "to ensure our democratic right to protest and our safety."

The event invitation even included safety tips for attendees, a number to dial in case of medical emergency, and instructions on how to spot the trained legal observers who would be present to document potential provocateurs and any incidents that might occur.

The student body was organized and ready to carry out its peaceful protest, as had so many others outside Sproul Hall over the decades.

But somehow everything went wrong. The violence intensified so rapidly that no one saw it coming. And no one knew exactly who or what was behind it. Even Sergeant Reich couldn't explain it.

People who have been to battle know that the most dangerous attacks don't announce their arrival. The most lethal attack is the one that catches us by surprise.

The military describes such blindness to impending attack as the "fog of war": the myriad things you may not know about your adversary—their location, numbers, capabilities, and goals.

But think about this: what if the fog not only denied you access to the facts but actually convinced you of the validity of erroneous data? From a business perspective, imagine not merely being unsure about the number of your customers but being certain of an *incorrect* number. It's under this condition— of believing wrong information—that the most difficult issues emerge and take us by surprise.

There is always some fog present, and organizations try to diffuse it as best they can.

The military uses on-the-ground scouts, communications intercepts, high-resolution satellites, and night-vision technology to track and assess the enemy. Businesses analyze market trends to identify and outmaneuver the competition. But what if the information you see deceives rather than informs you? The real danger in battle and in business "wars" is that you may be convinced you have a clear picture when you don't actually understand what you're seeing.

That's exactly what happened in Berkeley. Without anyone realizing it, the fog of war enveloped the campus. The attack wasn't at all what it appeared to be. This brings us back to our conversation with Sergeant Reich.

She, along with the rest of her police force, is dedicated to protecting the campus and the community. But in order to protect against an attack, you need to know who's waging it.

This fundamental question—who incited the Berkeley violence—has ramifications far beyond the Berkeley police or even the city itself. As Reich and her colleagues tried to make sense of what was happening during the protests, operatives from both political parties on the national level were composing their own narratives about what was going on.

When violence breaks out at a protest, fingers naturally point at the organizers themselves. But as we have noted, these particular organizers were of the nonviolent type. Gandhi could've learned a thing or two from them about organizing peacefully. Even if we're to believe that the culprits were the student organizers, who regardless of their co-op lives *did* turn violent, why would they target, of all the buildings on campus, the *student* building, the one that houses all the student clubs (which—wait for it—skew heavily progressive)?

It would be out of character for them to do so, they had no motive for targeting that part of campus, and they had no history of such behavior. Either something completely unexpected happened that morphed these peace-loving liberals into hyper-aggressive militants or there's more to the story.

That's exactly what Reich thought when she looked at the events. Something just didn't make sense. But if the student organizers didn't cause the violence, who did?

"We believe," Sergeant Reich told us, "that these were paid anarchists." If it sounds like a wild conspiracy theory, it is.

There is no evidence that anyone was paid, and no one knows anything about who these so-called anarchists even might be. But here's a Berkeley police sergeant admitting that this is her leading theory. At this point the only thing we can be certain of is that the fog of war lay thick on the city of Berkeley, drifting to cover everyone nationwide who was trying to make heads or tails of the situation.

But if paid anarchists were responsible for the Berkeley violence, who paid them? One narrative holds that the anarchists were paid by one of the far-left extremist groups behind the riot, Refuse Fascism, said to have received $50,000 from a group backed by socialist billionaire George Soros. The theory was that "anti-fascists" started several fires, smashed windows and ATMs, looted downtown stores, attacked cars, and assaulted dozens of Milo Yiannopoulos fans.

Why, though, would a left-leaning organization (and a respectable funder) hire thugs to vandalize arguably the most progressive university in the country?

This is where yet a third theory of events enters the picture. Under this theory, the anarchists weren't paid by the Left. Rather, Yiannopoulos and Breitbart were in cahoots with the agitators, laying the groundwork for a White House crackdown on liberal universities and their federal funding.

In a blog post about why the protests turned violent, Berkeley professors drew a connection among Yiannopoulos, Steve Bannon, and President Donald Trump, suggesting that the violence could have been coordinated to support the president's call during his campaign to revoke federal funding for UC Berkeley.

And thus we have three competing accounts, each troubling in its own right.

Were Berkeley students out of control?

Did communists pay agitators to vandalize the campus?

Or did conservatives and affiliated media stage a coordinated information operations campaign?

At least two of these theories had to be wrong, and one of them had to be right. Right? Maybe not. What if the police, the university professors, the government, and the media reported the events *as they saw them* but were *all* mistaken?

In trying to figure out who the perpetrators were that night, we discover a global trend and a battle being waged right under our noses but unrecognized by even the most careful of observers.

Uncle Shoe Store

At a family Christmas party, Ori found himself in a conversation with an uncle who's a professor of philosophy, specializing in language and epistemology. The two were talking about fake news and how in the near future the trend might affect our ability to discern the truth. Halfway through the conversation, they were joined by another uncle, a physical therapist who runs a specialty shoe store for athletes. This uncle is one of the top experts in the country on running shoes and even holds a patent on a machine that tests a shoe's stability to gauge its appropriateness for a given runner.

The conversation—as tends to happen at family events—turned to global affairs. Uncle Shoe Store mentioned that he'd read about a Harvard professor who demonstrated that climate change science is wrong. "I mean, look around," he continued. "It's not hot this winter in San Francisco."

Of course, Uncle Philosopher is at the opposite end of the

political spectrum, so Ori bit his tongue and sat back to watch the fireworks. Instead of engaging in an argument, Uncle Philosopher asked Uncle Shoe Store how he had reached his conclusions.

Uncle Shoe Store said that he had read the information online, and that a number of his friends—all successful business owners—had read and agreed with the same materials. Uncle Philosopher tried to ask about the multitude of peer-reviewed journal articles backing climate change, but Uncle Shoe Store put little stock in them.

Just as Ori kept his mouth shut at Christmas, we're not going to weigh in on climate change. For a moment, though, let's view Uncle Shoe Store from the perspective of someone who believes in climate change.

We need to recognize that Uncle Shoe Store isn't simply spouting unfounded beliefs. He is actually being rational—reading up on climate change in his favorite publications, seeing what the people he trusts on social media say, etc., and coming to a rational (albeit debatable) conclusion. He's in no way irrational. He's reached a conclusion based on both the data in front of him and the so-called wisdom of the crowd. In other words, not only does he find the data compelling, but he's verifying it via a statistically established methodology. He's just not necessarily aware that the crowd whose wisdom he's tapping may be decidedly biased.

As much as we might feel superior to someone who holds an alternative view of scientific data, we *all* are soon going to suffer the same fate. What Uncle Shoe Store didn't account for as he gathered information and formed judgments was the digital echo. He wasn't alone.

There soon will come a time when, despite using all the resources available to us, we will simply not be able to tell what is actually true. This, as we'll soon see, is what happened at the Berkeley protest. Let's look at two other examples.

First, consider a recent hoax in which, with the aid of bots, the Twitterverse was convinced that a Louisiana chemical plant had gone up in flames—local news even reported on the fire. They eventually got the facts right when they sent a reporter to the scene, but what happens when local news gets replaced by distributed networks?

In other words, what will happen when *anyone* can produce a news story? In a case like this false fire, social media might have two versions of the same story. One would say there was no fire—showing a video of the unburned site—and then there would be another narrative, with photos purporting to show the explosion and its victims.

Now, what does that mean for a future allegation of, say, the use of chemical weapons in Syria? Or of some kind of warfare engaged in by the U.S. government? Will the public be able to discern what is actually real?

In the second example, mal intent wasn't even a factor. On December 27, 2016 (two days after the family Christmas party), a protester threw some firecrackers at a government building in Bangkok. This triggered a Facebook alert for an "explosion" (based on an unnamed "trusted third party"), and users proceeded to mark themselves "safe." The Facebook alert linked to a news story that referenced BBC "breaking news" footage of an explosion in Bangkok . . . that had happened a year earlier. News outlets saw the BBC logo and, in their rush to cover what appeared to be a major breaking story, overlooked the date on the video and hastily posted their own stories about the explosion.[2]

Of course, the error was quickly discovered and the Facebook alert was taken down. In the old days, newspapers wouldn't even have had time to take the story to print, television news

---

2. *"Facebook Safety Check Creates False Alarm in Bangkok,"* BBC.com, *December 28, 2016, www.bbc.com/news/world-asia-38448140.*

outlets that covered it would have run a correction, and that would have been that. But with news traveling at the speed of links and clicks, news of the "explosion" spread around the globe within minutes—and continued to spread even after Facebook corrected its error. And so, if you Googled "December 27, 2016, bombing in Thailand," there was a good chance that your top search result would be a story based on inaccurate data.

It's not always accurate to call instances like these "fake news." They can occur without any intentional deception. An inaccurate news story—even an accidentally inaccurate one—creates a "digital echo," and though the original source may be corrected, the echo—reverberating across distributed networks—endures forever.

What Really Happened in Berkeley (We Think)

Recall that we had three competing narratives about who was responsible for the violence and vandalism at Berkeley. Our first narrative blamed the students, our second blamed anarchists paid by conservative institutions, and our third blamed the same anarchists—but had them paid by the far Left.

Unsatisfied with the UC Berkeley Police's explanation, Ori continued to dig. He talked to a student who used to work for U.S. intelligence but got no answers. He asked other faculty, but they were equally perplexed. Ultimately he remembered that one of his students had written a paper on anarchist structures and turned to him for insight.

The student didn't want to talk on the phone, so Ori met him at a dive restaurant near campus.

"So, do you have any info? Which narrative is correct?"

"None of them," the student said. "They're all wrong."

And so we present narrative four, as told by Ori's student.

Anarchists did indeed attend the protest. They smashed the windows of Amazon and bank outlets within the student center to express their dissatisfaction with the economic divide. They weren't paid by anyone—and in fact were so wary of being found out that they didn't even communicate via social media.

At some point during the night, a heat lamp fell down and caught fire. There were no Molotov cocktails. These kids didn't know how to make one.

But when the media reported that firebombs had been thrown, the UC Police thought the campus was actually under paramilitary attack. Instead of making arrests, they retreated in the face of what they believed to be a superior force. The situation therefore wasn't contained and continued to spiral out of control. In other words, the digital echo affected real-time police action, which allowed the situation to escalate.

We underscore that no law enforcement individuals acted negligently. Just like Uncle Shoe Store, they responded in a rational manner to the information presented to them. That information originated from unreliable sources but was quickly amplified by being retweeted, reposted, and repeated, to the point where it appeared legitimate.

They fell victim to the digital echo. It could happen to any of us.

In a world where verifying facts is becoming increasingly difficult, inclusion is imperative. It gives us sources as close to the ground or the action as possible, providing our best chance of getting at the truth.

Despite our best efforts, there will still be times when truth cannot be reliably distinguished from fiction. In the absence of verifiable truth, competing narratives will vie for allegiance. When we are forced to compete in a battle of narratives, inclusion is still our best weapon: only by leveraging a diversity of voices can we create a winning narrative.

CHAPTER 2: **THE POWER OF NARRATIVE**

McDonald's vs. McVegan

To begin our investigation, we remain on Sproul Plaza but go back in time.

Twenty-two years before the Milo Yiannopoulos protests, in 1995, Ori was pulling a metal wagon along Sproul, the very spot where the agitators—whoever they were—would wage their attack. Ori normally walks with a hurried stride, but you wouldn't have guessed it from his pace that day, which was nearly a crawl.

His load was heavy: two folding chairs, a card table, twenty stacks of pamphlets bound with thick blue rubber bands, and a dozen or so signs affixed to cardboard backing, all balanced atop a red wagon that had started its life as a toy for kids. Now, having been donated to the cause, it was covered in political stickers. The wagon's front left and rear right wheels wobbled under the weight of its cargo. *Tadamtumtruph, tadamtumtruph, tadamtumtruph*, they groaned as they rolled over the smallest bumps in the concrete.

There were also psychological reasons for Ori's slow pace. He wasn't just pulling a heavy wagon; he was feeling heavy as well. Simply put, he dreaded arriving at his destination a few hundred feet away on Sproul Plaza, along one of two rows where student clubs "tabled" about their particular causes.

He found an open spot between the lacrosse club and an environmental group.

Ori began by unfolding the card table, then organized the pamphlets into four neat rows. Pamphlets on animal research at Berkeley were in the first row, information about the abuse of primates in the second, the philosophical arguments for animal rights in the third, and miscellaneous pamphlets explaining the history of animal rights in the fourth.

Next he put up a poster for his group: a vivid photo of a chimpanzee strapped to a metal contraption with the block-letter words BERKELEY STUDENTS FOR ANIMAL LIBERATION underneath.

He sighed. It was time for the debates to start. Ironically, Ori had joined the group to meet new people. He was putting himself through college, and to save money, rather than splurge on a dorm room, he lived on the wrong side of town with a schizophrenic who spent nights arguing with the voices in his head.

A freshman living off campus and a committed vegan, Ori had hoped he'd meet like-minded friends. Instead, here he was engaging in a debate with a biochemistry PhD candidate about the efficacy of animal studies.

"You're all idealists who don't know what you're talking about," the scientist said, his voice rising.

Ori tried to take a reasoned approach, but the tension only mounted. Meanwhile, the guy at the lacrosse table was engaged in a lengthy conversation with a tanned freshman interested in joining intramural sessions.

How Ori wished he had joined lacrosse, or even the environmental club, where a group of hippies were talking about a beach cleanup project. At least those two groups *attracted* potential members.

Things came to a head a few weeks later, when BSAL organized its first protest of the semester. After doing rigorous recruiting, making special signs, and obtaining a permit from the city, BSAL staged a daylong protest outside a McDonald's. Out of the tens of thousands of Berkeley students, seven people showed up.

The tiny group held up signs showing photographs taken in slaughterhouses and gave out pamphlets describing the difficult conditions within them. The hope was that the graphic imagery would sway opinions. "Wait a second," a passer-by might say. "I respect animals and this place tortures them?"

That conversation never happened.

Instead people engaged Ori in so-called debates, which were more like one-sided tirades about why he was wrong and/or crazy. And those who didn't engage in such debates—the vast majority of people, that is—ignored him and his fellow protesters. And when we say ignore, we mean *ignore*. It was as if the animal rights activists were phantoms.

But Ori was undeterred.

By noon, the group had stood out in front of McDonald's for three hours. They had given out hundreds of flyers but hadn't actually dissuaded anyone from going in. Then a middle-aged woman, her kid in tow, walked toward the group.

She looked like she could be one of Ori's mom's friends: friendly and kind, a woman in whose home he could have grown up. The nice lady approached the group, and Ori and his peers smiled at her. *Finally, here's someone on our side*, they thought. But the woman said nothing. Instead she came up to the guy standing next to Ori and literally spit in his face.

As she walked away, she yelled toward the stunned protesters, "Stuck-up elitists!"

It was an ironic epithet to hurl at a group of activists who wore secondhand clothes and persisted primarily on lentils and cabbage. But at the same time, whatever you might think of the politeness of spitting in someone's face, the woman came from an understandable place.

Here she was trying to take her kid out for a fun, affordable meal, and a bunch of protesters were calling her immoral. Let's face it: health food *is* more expensive and difficult to find than ubiquitous McDonald's restaurants. What gave these holier-than-thou protesters the right to tell her what she should do?

If mothers were spitting at you, Ori reasoned, clearly something needed to change. He realized that he and his fellow BSAL members were losing the debate.

Over the next months, they put the protests on hold and strategized about how to actually make a difference—how to get through to the people they were trying to reach. The group came up with a number of ideas for new tactics, but Ori realized that no matter what they did, BSAL couldn't compete with groups like the lacrosse club. It just wasn't as . . . fun.

Then one evening Ori and his friend Leor Jacobi allowed themselves to dream.

"Imagine if we opened up a veggie burger place across from McDonald's," Ori said.

"With an even better playground outside," Leor added.

"Yeah," Ori continued. "We'd call it McVegan."

There was a pause. A smile spreading across his face, Leor said, "We can do that."

"Open a restaurant?" Ori asked.

"No, create the parody." Leor spoke with alacrity. "Give veggie burgers away on Sproul."

Leor sat down at his Mac that night and stayed glued to Photoshop for the next couple of days. The design he came up with featured the famous golden arches, but instead of the familiar slogan, it read "McVegan: Billions and Billions Saved."

It's important to note that just a few years earlier, unless he worked at an ad agency, Leor wouldn't have had access to a computer able to perform this design work. But now, working in his little room at home, what he produced was . . . perfect.

McVegan represented a new tactic: create a positive narrative around being vegan. Being vegan is fun! It's hip! All your friends are doing it! The next day Ori, Leor, and their friend Mark Schlosberg started vegan.org.

It was also the day that Ori killed BSAL. Immediately the president of every major animal rights group called him to yell at him: "You're killing the animal rights movement!"

"Yes, that's the idea," he responded.

It wasn't that he had anything against animal rights; it was just that he'd realized that the debate *couldn't* be won because of the barriers it erected.

For one thing, scientists who used animals in their labs could not, by definition, be a part of the movement. That left an entire group—a group of very smart people, many of whom conducted their research in hopes of helping other people by curing a disease or gaining knowledge about health—inherently excluded. What's more, in a debate about morality and the role of animals, could you say *for sure* that you were right and that the other side was wrong?

Let's pause for a moment. Ask yourself, how many times during your personal or professional life have you been on the right side of an argument but been unable to convince others around you?

How many teams have you been a part of that felt excluded from the overall organization?

And even if you've never held a protest sign in your life, how many times have you felt that you were speaking to deaf ears?

Now imagine what a pain it was to teach people about veganism, of all things.

Remember that at the time, in the mid-1990s, very few people even knew the word "vegan." This was long before the numerous studies showing the benefits of a plant-based diet. Most people knew that vegetarianism meant not eating animals, but vegans avoid *all* animal-derived products—no eggs, dairy, or leather.

To add to the challenges, "vegan" is not exactly a melodious word that rolls off your tongue. It's a branding choice no marketing person would ever come up with. Ori realized that either he could earnestly make the case for giving up animal products or he could take a page from McDonald's book.

The objective of McVegan was to make veganism inclusive—even of nonvegans. Rather than engage in a debate, it created a narrative where veganism was palatable, fun, even funny. If the fast food chain was using clowns and playgrounds to promote its food, why couldn't Ori do the same?

Wearing T-shirts bearing the golden arches and accompanied by the McVegan mascot, Reggie McVeggie, Ori's group gave out free veggie burgers. And after months and months of tabling for animal rights only to be ignored, suddenly the McVegan stand was mobbed by curious students.

Within an hour, they had given out more than a thousand veggie burgers. Moreover, even nonvegans, ye olde carnivores, loved the T-shirts so much that they asked to buy them. All of a sudden people loved the activists; veganism was becoming a cool, fun counterculture movement. And no one was spitting in anyone's face.

Leor and Ori printed colorful T-shirts and stickers and started selling them to punk-rock kids at concerts. The kids would stick them on their shoes, their bikes, their hats. The logo was becoming a fun fashion accessory.

One day Ori spotted a kid on a bike with a McVegan sticker.

"Did you get that at Gilman?" he asked the kid.

"At where?" the kid answered, unaware of the alternative

venue where punk rock bands like Green Day performed before they made it big. "No, dude, I got it from my friend. He gave it to me because I work at McDonald's."

McVegan was equally appealing to punk rockers, to people who didn't like the idea of corporate fast food, to kids who wanted to rebel, and to those who just thought it was funny. You could wear a McVegan T-shirt and still eat a Big Mac.

Soon other colleges held their own McVegan events, inspired by the narrative.

But not everyone thought it was funny.

Many of Ori's friends in the environmental movement argued that McVegan still encouraged consumerism. They argued that McVegan belittled a serious issue. The fact that someone could wear a T-shirt and still consume meat was evidence, they argued, that the path to societal change was to defend the facts and work toward policy changes.

The other folks who weren't amused, unsurprisingly, were McDonald's executives and lawyers. Just as McVegan was gaining a little bit of attention, McDonald's threatened to sue for trademark infringement.

Uh-oh.

How can you possibly win a legal battle against McDonald's? Leor, Ori, and Mark huddled and ultimately made the decision based on their bicycles. Specifically, the bikes were pretty much their only possessions, so what did they have to lose?

They decided to fight back, but not in the way you'd expect. They realized that, unlike their previous protests, this wouldn't be a debate.

McVegan and Reggie McVeggie were literal clowns who were causing McDonald's a whole lot of grief. At that point, McDonald's had to make a choice. The natural inclination—the obvious strategy—was to get rid of the clowns, to silence them.

Indeed, that's what McDonald's tried to do. That's when

something weird happened. By attacking McVegan, McDonald's was only shining light on Reggie McVeggie, only giving him more prominence and inadvertently *amplifying* the narrative. And McVegan was simply more *fun* and more *hip* than McDonald's.

All of a sudden T-shirt and sticker orders were coming in from around the world.

That's when Ori had a fundamental realization: as the underdog, it's easier to engage in a war of narratives than it is to win a debate on the merits.

Because McVegan was inclusive, because anyone could be a part of it, there was no one (other than McDonald's) who was terribly offended by it or set against it. After a number of positive news stories broke, reporters were calling to get the McVegan side of the story. But rather than engage in a debate, Ori dressed up as Reggie McVeggie and held a press conference.

The next day McDonald's dropped its case.

Now, what if McDonald's had chosen a different strategy? Rather than trying to win the debate, what if it had recognized that it was engaged in a *battle of narratives*?

This is the first major element of the new environment shaping our world. Narratives, as we'll see, are having greater and greater impact in industries and on the world political stage alike. More specifically, the world is moving from debates about facts to battles of narratives.

Facts are about being right or wrong. McDonald's believed it was wrong for McVegan to have infringed the trademark. But narratives aren't as concerned with who is right and who is wrong; they're focused on who's more *interesting*.

Facts are by definition grounded in logic. Narratives, however, are based on emotions. McVegan wasn't about whether it's logical to eat a beef burger or a soy alternative. It was simply declaring that the alternative was fun. McVegan was powerful in the same way that a clown in a circus has power, or a jester in a royal court. A jester could mock the king by distilling one attribute, twisting it, and giving it a new (and funny) interpretation. Reggie McVeggie gave a new spin to Ronald McDonald: what if healthy eating were fun?

Facts need to be verified in order to have utility. But narratives gain power merely by spreading. Each punk-rock kid who put a McVegan sticker on his or her bike to protest commercialism spread the narrative; as did each McDonald's employee who did so as a joke. Thus McVegan mutated and could be both a critique of fast food *and* a good-natured spoof.

Unlike facts, no one expects narratives to be exacting. They are *derivatives* of the truth, not pure versions of it. Thus they're allowed to be more flexible and agile, because they spread by being interesting, not necessarily by being accurate. They don't have to be scientifically on point; they just need to have a compelling plot.

This brings us to the core of the issue. Facts depend on expert validation to persist, while narratives simply need to be retold. That means that you can't win a narrative battle by simply proving that the opposing narrative is in some way inaccurate. *A narrative battle is won by drowning out the countermessage.*

Imagine if instead of viewing McVegan and Reggie McVeggie as adversaries to be silenced, McDonald's had taken a page from Shakespeare's King Lear, who noted that "jesters do oft prove prophets." In other words, what if McVegan was onto an emerging trend?

Indeed, while Ori hasn't done any work on McVegan since 1995, the concept endured. In 2015 industry publication *AgWeb* posted an article with a title that would have seemed impossible two decades earlier: "McVegan: Former McDonald's CEO Joining Board of Beyond Meat" (a veggie burger maker). Don Thompson, former McDonald's CEO, had turned veggie burger enthusiast.

It wasn't necessarily that Thompson had a philosophical

change of heart about burgers—rather, he was following market demands. He wasn't the only business executive who warmed up to veggie burgers. Bill Gates joined a version of the McVegan campaign as well. More on that later. The point is that veganism, thanks to inclusive narratives, is no longer on the fringe of society. In fact, just a few weeks before this book went to press, news broke that McDonald's itself was testing a new vegan burger. Its name? The McVegan.[3]

What if McDonald's had *amplified* rather than tried to squelch McVegan, and what if *it* had developed the veggie burger first and capitalized on that market potential?

The argument here isn't that we should welcome various ideas—even those that are seemingly clownish and out of left field—for the sake of being "nice." Rather, through inclusion companies can both react to market forces that are demanding a voice and stay competitive. Think how much easier it would have been for McDonald's to tap its marketing team instead of its lawyers, boosting the McVegan message—even celebrating it—and bringing the narrative under McDonald's own tent.

Facts	Narratives
Right or wrong	Interesting or boring
Logical	Emotional
Verified	Spread
Stay rigid	Easily mutate
Precise truth	Approximation of truth
Objective	Subjective
Depend on experts	Depend on retelling
Countered by disproving	Countered by drowning out
Tendency to exclude	Tendency to include

3. Andrea Park, *"McDonald's Unveils Vegan Burger in Finland,"* Bon Appetit, *October 6, 2017, www.bonappetit.com/story/mcdonalds-vegan-burger-finland.*

This idea of broadening one's scope to be more inclusive in the quest for greater effectiveness is what led to this book. It's what led General Dempsey to reach out to a peace-studies-Berkeley-teaching-tofu-eating person like Ori to get his help improving the U.S. military's ability to function effectively.

The Resolute *Desk*

Presidential administrations have come and gone, but the same desk—crafted from the timbers of the British ship HMS *Resolute* and gifted by Queen Victoria to President Rutherford B. Hayes in 1880—has remained a fixture of the Oval Office since the days of JFK.

Kennedy sat at the *Resolute* desk when he deliberated how to deal with the Cuban missile crisis in 1962, and it was at that desk that he famously authorized the embargo of Cuba; it was at the same desk in 1987 that Ronald Reagan negotiated the terms of a nuclear disarmament deal with Russia.

It was there, in 2013, that President Obama faced an issue no less challenging than the ones JFK and Reagan had to overcome.

Just a few days before that Tuesday afternoon in April 2013, spring announced itself with the full glory of the cherry blossoms in bloom. But now the mood in D.C., and in the country as a whole, had shifted dramatically.

It had been less than two hours since the terrorist attack at the Boston Marathon.

The president immediately assembled his closest national security advisers at a closed-door meeting.

As he waited for the president to enter the Oval Office, General Dempsey looked to his right at Chuck Hagel, the secretary of defense. Hagel was straightening his tie, and when he caught Dempsey's look, he slowly shook his head and sighed heavily. National Security Advisor Susan Rice, on his left, buried her nose in her briefing book, poring over the intelligence reports she had recently received.

Every administration has its ups and downs, but the nine months leading up to that meeting in April had seen one vexing national security issue after another. Dempsey knew that there would be intense interest in determining the motivation behind this new attack on American soil.

He had received news of the bombing when his executive officer, Colonel John Novalis, interrupted his preparations for his testimony before Congress, scheduled for the next day. Novalis had just completed a tour of duty as commander of an attack aviation brigade in Afghanistan. He had been selected because he was combat tested, virtually unflappable, and an exceptional leader. Dempsey knew Novalis would interrupt him only with something important.

"Sir, there's been an incident," Novalis said.

From his executive officer's demeanor Dempsey could tell that what he was working on would have to wait.

"There's been an attack on the Boston Marathon," Novalis continued, then explained as concisely and clearly as possible that there had been two explosions near the finish line of the Boston Marathon and that the attackers were still at large. The Joint Staff Intelligence Officer and Joint Staff Operations Officer were meeting and would come to him with their assessment in the next fifteen minutes.

While most of us will never bear the awesome responsibility of defending our nation's security, many of us have been in a situation where the status quo is suddenly disrupted. Dempsey had been trained over a lifetime to respond to exactly these kinds of crises.

He knew that the secretary of defense and the president would soon summon their national security teams, and he must be prepared. Indeed, ninety minutes later he was in the Oval Office. The media was already speculating about whether the attack was a result of U.S. withdrawal from the Middle East and whether it represented a new, previously hidden threat to the country's safety. All of that would play out over time. Right now Dempsey needed to assure the president that the military was engaged, ready, and vigilant.

A quiet moment passed before the Oval Office door swung open, admitting a clamor—a staff member in conversation with the head of the FBI, several phones ringing, interns talking in rapid succession.

President Obama entered the room, loosened his tie, and rolled up his sleeves. In less than two hours he would address the nation on live TV. He looked for a place to sit but instead headed straight to the *Resolute* desk, leaned on its corner, and directed his first question to Dempsey. "Marty, give us your perspective."

Most of us haven't spent a day in uniform, but from watching Hollywood movies it's easy to assume the head of the U.S. military would be a hawk, constantly pushing for aggressive combat operations. In reality, however, in the past ten years Dempsey had learned much about both the capabilities and the limitations of military power.

Nevertheless, he had to lay out all the options for the president. He had been with the president in other crises and knew that what he valued in these situations was clarity and brevity.

"Mr. President," Dempsey began, "military personnel are providing support to law enforcement officials in Massachusetts. As you know, the Massachusetts National Guard has mobilized several hundred troops. We're coordinating closely with the Department of Homeland Security.

"The Global Response Force remains at its normal state of readiness. We will accelerate their readiness time lines," he continued, explaining that key parts of the military were being placed on high alert. "There are several things I will recommend if we receive intelligence that indicates the attack was part of a larger coordinated campaign or if it is accompanied by an increase of hostile activity toward our interests overseas. These could include ordering Strategic Command to maneuver satellite coverage and Cyber Command to shift assets to reinforce the FBI and Department of Homeland Security. It's too soon to tell for sure, but at this time it appears that the attack is an isolated event."

Privately, though, Dempsey wondered whether intelligence would link the perpetrators of this attack to any particular terrorist group. And then he wondered if that really mattered anymore. He looked at the *Resolute* desk a few feet away and reflected on how many obstacles it had seen overcome, how many changes it had borne witness to during its time in the Oval Office. Over the next few weeks and months, it would become obvious that we were experiencing something transformative.

Unlike the perpetrators of previous terrorist acts in the United States, the Tsarnaev brothers never received in-person training—neither at a camp nor through a network. This is where the threads of our story converge in an interesting way. Could it be that in order to fully understand what happened in Boston—and, for that matter, what happened at the Berkeley Milo Yiannopoulos protests—we need to look at the world through a McVegan lens?

Exactly two years after the Boston Marathon bombings, Ori convened a meeting at Harvard Business School where he invited senior White House officials, entrepreneurs, members of the Islamic community, media strategists, and policy experts to discuss how we might prevent an attack like the one in Boston from happening again.

The group began by trying to understand how the Tsarnaev brothers were recruited to commit the terror acts in the first place. They weren't part of a formal organization that gave them commands, nor were they even members of an underground network that hatched a September 11–style attack.

In fact, the successful war against such terror networks had parallels, in a weird way, to what happened with Berkeley Students for Animal Liberation.

Like BSAL, starved for members, the terror networks had turned to technology and to narratives to stay alive. Just as Ori created McVegan shirts and stickers, terror group members were posting their content online and hoping for the best.

In the past several years, more and more videos had been posted. And remember: top-ranked videos are by definition compelling and easy to mutate or, more specifically, regenerate. The narrative continued to mutate until the Tsarnaev brothers learned from that content and committed their act of terror.

In a very real way, the narrative had *become* the organization.

The Harvard group recognized that you couldn't contain the narratives through conventional means. Eliminating them from one social media site was like playing Whack-a-Mole, as videos would pop up on another site almost instantaneously. Trying to debunk the message (and win the debate) only gave the videos more attention.

That same year, a Palestinian stabbed a bus driver in Tel Aviv and posted the act of terror online. The terrorist had no organizational affiliation, and the video wasn't promoted by a group of people. Still, viewers were inspired to commit their own stabbings and post these new derivative videos online.

Of course, positive content can spread in the same way; think of the "It Gets Better" campaign. But just as after 9/11 we had to get our heads around the fact that a distributed network—lacking a leader and without infrastructure—was a force to be reckoned with, we now needed to start considering videos and other narrative-building content as their *own entities*.

This brings us back to UC Berkeley. What if the protesters were actually organized neither by centralized command-and-control organizations nor by distributed networks, but instead were led, actually led, by online videos?

Online videos make it easy to belong, to feel an affiliation with a story, especially a memorable one. Lacking resources, the weaker player will often resort to fighting a narrative battle because—unlike court cases or massive protests—producing a story is cheap and easy.

The Web and social media mean that virtually anyone can post a video story. Instead of relying on centralized distribution channels, video stories are easily disseminated among members of a network and beyond.

All of these factors give video stories their own digital version of life. Think, for a moment, of a YouTube or Facebook video as a living organism.

The more people watch the video, the more money the companies make, so the success of a video is measured in views or shares, and successful videos are promoted and thus make their way to even more eyeballs. To this end, a video "tries" to sustain itself through being watched and "tries" to keep the family line "alive" by the same means plants and animals do: it mutates and reproduces.

A popular video that encourages the creation of derivative content "lives" on through its descendants. In other words, video stories want to be as compelling as possible and as mutable (and replicable) as possible.

Back at Harvard, the realization that narratives had become a new type of organization also shed light on how governments and businesses alike can react to a market force that demands inclusion.

Coal-Rollin' a Prius:
The Market Conditions for Inclusion

"I came over here because it was quiet!" shouted the Prius driver, apparently oblivious to the contrast between her words and her actions.

Dressed in all black, a blue cellphone in her left hand, the woman looked through her glasses with contempt. She was apparently angry at the driver of the pickup truck idling next to her in the parking lot.

"There was nobody here," the woman continued, "and you come up here with your gas-guzzling piece of s*** and your exhaust spewing everywhere."

Alarmed by the Prius driver's words and demeanor, the pickup driver immediately thought of her kids. Well, actually, first she picked up her phone to record the interaction. "Hey," she said in a calm voice that would quickly turn heated, "don't you swear in front of my daughter."

From there the situation escalated. "Shut the f*** up," the Prius driver responded. "You're mindless and you're ignorant."

The video, shot in 2014, went viral, gaining millions of views. The fact that the video went viral isn't all that surprising. After all, it showed a juicy conflict involving an apparent elitist scolding an apparently working-class driver in ways that were crass enough you couldn't help but watch.

Prius owners are, on average, more wealthy, more likely to have a college education, and therefore perhaps more, well, elitist. In California, paying more for a Prius than an average family car affords drivers access to the carpool lane and exudes a certain air of status. You can't show up to a venture capital meeting in a beat-up truck, but you can certainly show up in a Prius.

What was truly surprising was what happened as a result of the video spreading. All of a sudden, it took on a life of its own.

As the Prius video continued to spread, local news reporters from across the country informed audiences about a new trend taking the streets and YouTube by storm. They called it "rolling coal."

For decades diesel truck drivers had experimented with modifications to their trucks in order to emit additional clouds of sooty exhaust into the air. Prior to the summer of 2014, videos of the practice existed on YouTube with little to no viewership, and most consisted mainly of a tricked-out truck whizzing past an enthusiastic amateur cameraman as thick black smoke emerged from the truck's tailpipe or ancillary smokestack.

But in July 2014 the EPA announced that the practice of rolling coal violated the Clean Air Act, which prohibits the manufacture, sale, or installation of any part of a motor vehicle that tampers with emission-control devices. Diesel truck drivers turned to YouTube to make a political statement in response.

Within days of the announcement, coal-rolling videos became a viral phenomenon. Videos took such forms as "coal-rollin' on a hot girl," where a male driver would pull up next to a female pedestrian, leeringly ask if she smoked, then blow a cloud of soot on the unsuspecting woman. Another variety involved a coal-rolling supporter placing his or her face inches from the tailpipe of a parked diesel truck while a friend mashed the accelerator. One of the video's most popular forms was "smoke attacks" on Priuses and their drivers.

Each video and its slight variations served as lifeblood for the overall anti-Prius narrative.

A group of coal-rollers even took a road trip to put some Prius-drivin' progressives in their place. They drove to, you guessed it, Berkeley and coal-rolled an anti-Trump rally.

Now, think about this from Toyota's perspective. The spread of the coal-rolling narrative was bad for the Prius brand on two levels. First, every time coal-rolling gained a new fan, that was one more person who would never, ever, ever consider buying a Prius, no matter how well built, reliable, sleek, or environmentally friendly it might be. And imagine the derision coal-rolling enthusiasts would heap on anyone in their circle of acquaintance who bought one. Second, especially in regions where coal-rolling was really taking off, it could dissuade car shoppers who might otherwise consider a Prius. After all, who wants to be a target for that sort of thing?

What could Toyota have done to combat the coal-rolling narrative? Certainly no slick national ad campaign would do the trick. We'll soon see that for companies wanting to effectively engage in a battle of narratives, inclusion is becoming the new way of being heard.

PART 2

HARNESSING THE
POWER OF INCLUSION

CHAPTER 3: **THE ECONOMICS OF INCLUSION: PARTICIPATION, PERSONALIZATION, AND PURPOSE**

In 2004 Maria Sipka sold her possessions in Australia, consolidated her real estate holdings, and packed two suitcases. She wanted to see the world.

The daughter of Eastern European immigrants, she grew up in a household where dialogue about a variety of subjects, exchange of ideas, and community were paramount. One's job, as a member of her family, was to connect with others and try to have a meaningful interaction. Nearly a year into her trip abroad, she found herself in exactly this type of conversation with a seventeen-year-old who pulled a rickshaw in Mumbai.

This serendipitous connection with the rickshaw driver will eventually lead us to understand how in order to effectively communicate our message, in order to actually be *heard*, we need to leverage inclusion.

Although her new connection slept in his rickshaw and sustained himself on scavenged food, Maria found in him a kindred spirit. "This young man had so much fire in his eyes," she told us. "My parents were refugees, and we had the same hunger." He had interests and ambitions far beyond his life as a rickshaw driver, but his lack of education and his economic background conspired to bar him from access to market resources and to many sources of information.

Then Maria asked herself a question that would have ramifications on the rest of her life and large implications for our investigation here. She thought to herself, *How do I have an impact on this person?*

Seeing an opportunity—to connect individuals like the rickshaw kid with others who shared their passions and curiosity—Maria cofounded Xing, a European social networking site that allowed people to come together in groups dedicated to particular causes or interests.

"When people congregate in online communities," she reflected, "they do so around their passion points. The more you exchange with people, the more trust you build, and the more opportunities come up."

"I got a taste of the potential for networks to revolutionize how people connect around the planet," she told us. "We had thousands of people who joined groups around a shared topic. They were investing five to ten hours a week into nurturing their audiences," she explained. After running the data, she came to a fundamental realization: "People who belonged to groups were nine times more likely to return to the platform."

These thriving communities enabled Xing to monetize the community, charging companies for advertisements—be it to find candidates for a job opening or to introduce a new product—targeted to particular segments of the network. Maria took the company public in Germany in 2006, and by 2017 its stock had quintupled in value and the company was worth well over a billion dollars.

The social network was minting money, and its advertisers were acquiring new customers. But many of the network's members, though they were finding meaning in the communities, couldn't reap the economic rewards of the network. (It's not as if there are a lot of online advertisers trying to hire rickshaw pullers.) The architects, the caretakers, the backbones of the community weren't getting any of the revenue. They were developing close bonds with one another but were feeling marginalized, even though they were in reality a part of the majority.

(Such sidelining, we should note, creates "target-rich" environments for videos like those disseminated by ISIS. To be clear, users don't join ISIS because they're feeling disenfranchised on YouTube. Rather, YouTube enables people to bond over feeling excluded in broader ways. Think back, for example, to the pickup drivers who felt sidelined by the Prius owner; they felt attacked simply for driving the wrong kind of vehicle.)

Here's where Maria Sipka recognized an untapped market opportunity that will help us understand the economics of inclusion: if you're able to give a marginalized community (be it a group of voters, the employees of a company, or a segment of social media users) a chance to participate, to personalize the content, and to do so toward a common purpose, you can tap into an underutilized resource that can be harnessed very effectively using fewer resources.

If ISIS could leverage videos to sign up recruits, why couldn't the same technology be used for good, providing community members with a revenue source and enabling businesses to better communicate with their audiences?

"We started talking to all the group leaders," Maria recalled, "and they told us, 'We are not marketers. Can you help us connect with sponsors? We need to feed our members some sort of experiences.'"

"On the flip side," she continued, "all these big brands, like

IBM and Cisco, are coming to us saying, 'We want to reach your members within the group.'" These companies were looking to place ads carefully designed by advertising agencies to appeal to certain segments of Xing users.

They were following the traditional economics of advertising: exert as much control as possible in order to deliver just the right message to the target consumer. To potential customers, however, the end result of this traditional advertising often felt more like bombardment than anything else.

Recognizing this, Maria decided to run an experiment. She partnered with Dove, which had just launched a campaign that ditched pencil-thin models and instead featured models who reflected how most women *actually* looked. Dove was doing a good job at developing content that mirrored its users; Maria had the idea to let community members actually *create* the content.

The notion of recruiting influencers to pitch a product isn't new. Think of an athlete endorsing a pair of sneakers. "You have Oprah and Kim Kardashian, who command $100,000 for mentioning a product in a single post," Maria explained. "Then you have admirers who adore your brand. We decided to focus on the micro-influencers."

Maria started including community builders who had previously been left out of the equation—in this case, stay-at-home moms. "They have a passion point that overlaps with the brand."

In partnership with Dove, those micro-influencers developed content about what beauty meant to them, and shared it with their communities. They would earn a little money every time someone clicked on the ad featuring their content. A few weeks later, Maria reviewed the results. When she looked at the hard numbers, she recalled, "I was like, there must be something wrong there." The numbers were so good that they were difficult to believe.

"Ads at the time had a 0.01% click-through rate," she explained to us. "Direct response was 1–2%. When that [micro-influencer-created] piece of content from Dove was unleashed onto those group members, we saw a 25% response rate. So I test it again, and it's right. What blew me away was that not only did we get the group leader to tell the story to create the advertisement, but the members not only watched the video, they started creating the commentary around the videos, and these conversations lasted for days and weeks. You have a decentralized conversation that carries on the original message."

In a sense, this is the bright side of the digital echo.

This simple change—bringing in the micro-influencers— created a new opportunity to reach consumers, and to do so more effectively and at a lower cost. Maria cofounded Linqia Influencer Marketing based on this concept.

Jon Pollack, Maria's vice president of product, explained the challenges the firm faced in this new age of the digital echo. "What excited me from a computer science engineering background is that this is a very challenging big-data problem. How do you get in front of everyone [the entire audience for a brand]? Originally it was a few TV networks. And then it became dozens. And then websites. When you move into an influencer space, everyone is potentially a leader of a community. The number of conduits and touch points has exploded over this trajectory. If there are millions of people who we can call community leaders or influencers, who do we pick to pair with a brand? The brand wants to make sure that the spokesperson knows the brand well, and the influencer can't be authentic if the brand doesn't fit into the needs of the members."

Maria added, "Whether you connect a group of scientists in Germany with a group of farmers in Botswana, it's through the community leaders and the decentralized approach that the entire power of the planet exists. Before, it used to be UN, big media, UNICEF. But now the key to influence is with these group leaders, because they're the ones who have the intimate connection with their audience. And then companies can leverage these storytellers. They become the creators of the story. They distribute the story in a highly decentralized way. Instead of going through a handful of media channels, we are going to activate fifty of these leaders, and they're all going to use their already-built channels to create content that's highly nuanced to their audience. And it'll happen within a week. And it won't cost millions."

This brings us to three central points of this book.

First, *not* including—exerting control—comes at an economic cost, one that is increasingly difficult to bear and harder still to justify.

Second, the way to thrive in the age of the digital echo is to bring a cause to a preexisting community. That is, rather than trying to build a community around a specific idea or belief, identify existing communities with whom the cause will likely resonate.

Third, and most important, although much has been written about diversity and the importance of inviting more people—and more voices—to the table, many of us have been viewing inclusion through the wrong lens. Inclusion isn't necessarily the opposite of exclusion. Real inclusion isn't about letting just anyone in; it's about understanding the pillars of **participation, personalization, and purpose.** We will catch up with Maria Sipka soon and see how she, and her company Linquia, have been able to make inclusion into a competitive advantage. But first let's go along on a secret mission General Dempsey embarked on during his time as head of the U.S. Army's leadership and training.

Participation: *The General's Secret Mission Leads to the Nevada Desert*

In 2009 U.S. Army General Martin Dempsey made a secret visit to a combat outpost nestled in the mountains along Afghanistan's border with Pakistan. He made the trip because he recognized that something was preventing him from seeing the actual state of events; the surprise he was about to encounter would permanently change how he viewed the world.

Dempsey had begun his trip more than seven thousand miles away, at his headquarters in Virginia. He was constantly briefed on minute details of the ongoing operations in Afghanistan, but he knew that he needed to show up in person and see things firsthand in order to completely understand everything. At Bagram Air Base the general transferred to a Blackhawk helicopter for the trip to the outpost. The smell of its fuel and sound of its rotors instantly took him back to his previous deployments, and he remembered what it was like being away from home, not knowing when this war would come to an end.

He had chosen to visit this remote outpost because just a few days earlier approximately twenty American soldiers there had been involved in a significant firefight with fifty to seventy-five Taliban fighters.

From his helicopter, the general could see the Himalayan mountains towering to the north and vast flatlands extending to the south. But his attention was focused on the mountains and hills directly below. There, hidden among jagged rock formations, sparse vegetation, and scattered villages of only a few mud buildings, were narrow trails winding along the mountainsides: an unimaginably harsh environment in which to live, let alone fight.

The trails below were thousands of years old, part of an ancient network of smuggling routes along Afghanistan's eastern border. In another time and on another day they would have been fascinating to study for the history and culture they would reveal.

But for the past ten years they had served as a continuous and effective supply chain providing the Taliban food, weapons, and ammunition. And at a critical "choke point," a small hilltop that dominated the route, a group of American soldiers were determined to interrupt this supply chain.

As the chopper prepared to land, the general spotted familiar faces from his advance team that had arrived the previous day. Standing next to them, shielding his eyes from the rotor wash of the descending helicopter, was the company commander, an army captain.

This twenty-eight-year-old officer was in charge of more than a hundred men spread over several different combat outposts, each facing its own unique challenges.

The captain was flanked by a dozen or so of his subordinates, who snapped to attention when Dempsey stepped out of the helicopter but didn't salute him, as they understood that, from somewhere in the surrounding hills, they were being watched.

The captain extended his hand in greeting. His grip was firm and his eyes revealed an unmistakable inner confidence and determination.

To put this encounter in context, this captain and his men would have been more likely to run into Michael Jordan playing a pickup basketball game in a local park than to have a substantive conversation with a four-star general. There are only ten four-star generals in the U.S. Army. To see a four-star this far downrange was a rarity, especially in the midst of a situation so unstable.

Put yourself in the captain's shoes. You were in a fight for your life just a few days ago, and now you have to brief a general. Are you nervous? Are you excited? Or, more likely, are you doing your best to simply not screw up?

Dempsey knew a lot about the situation on the ground, but he was here to figure out what he didn't know. In the early days of this war, in Baghdad, he had established a reputation for driving his subordinates to seek complexity rather than settle for simplicity.

Here on the eastern edge of the mission in Afghanistan, he wanted to learn from this captain how to deal with the complexity of smuggling routes along Afghanistan's border. If your opponent is bringing supplies via rail, you take out a few bridges, blow up a few kilometers of track, and you stave them off for a time. But here, when the army managed to block one path, smugglers would find a new one the next day. When one group of mercenaries was stopped, another would take its place.

The captain led the way to the eastern edge of the combat outpost, perched on a hilltop and half the size of a football field. Along the way, Dempsey took note of the dirt-filled Hesco bastions that provided a makeshift fence around the outpost. The captain had also moved several six-man "duck and cover" concrete shelters into the outpost for protection against mortar and rocket fire, and these were positioned near the plywood huts that the soldiers used for shelter.

This outpost was every bit of fifty kilometers from the nearest big forward operating base (FOB) with amenities like hot food, chemical toilets, showers, and Internet access. There were no such conveniences out here, Dempsey knew. The men here rotated back and forth to the bigger base camp every week or so. When they did so, it was always by helicopter, as the routes between the two American camps were among the most dangerous in Afghanistan.

At the eastern edge of the outpost was a plywood guard tower fifteen feet tall, extending about four feet above the Hesco bastions. The inside of the guard tower was lined with sandbags. Dempsey negotiated the eight rungs of the wooden ladder leading up to the guard tower. He could sense that his security team was a little nervous—not about the enemy but about the condition of the ladder. Dempsey winked at his lead security officer, a giant of a man nicknamed "Ox," as he headed up. Ox had been with him for three years and would stay with him through the remainder of his career.

The view from the guard tower was spectacular. It overlooked a small valley probably three kilometers across. The combat outpost was at eight thousand feet elevation; the mountains across the valley rose up to at least fourteen thousand feet. It had the feel of looking into a great wall.

Two trails emerged from the massive earth wall and converged in the center of the valley floor at a small village of ten mud huts. Only one trail emerged from the village; it passed to the left of the outpost at a distance of about a thousand meters. There was no other way out of this valley, which is why the location of this combat post was so integral and also why it was an object of such aggressive attention by the Taliban.

Dempsey climbed down from the tower and walked back with the captain to his makeshift office. Sitting across from the junior officer, Dempsey said, "Okay, Captain, here's your chance to influence not only your own part of the mission in Afghanistan but our entire strategy. What's going on? Tell me why you're here. What's your mission? Do you have the resources you need? Do you have the information you need? And most importantly, has anything surprised you?"

As it turned out, this captain had already figured out an ingenious way to make progress in his area of responsibility. "I've come to learn that I need to assess the outcome of my actions in the context of how they're understood by the local population," he told Dempsey. That is, achieving your mission—say, destroying part of the smuggling route, the system of trails—might bring significant military advantage, but if these actions disadvantaged the local population, they would ultimately make the mission impossible to achieve.

Put another way, the same mission outcomes could be simultaneously viewed as a victory and a setback. An analyst at the Pentagon might be pleased that a route was cut off, but if it was perceived by the locals as disrupting legitimate trade, destruction of the road would turn the locals against American forces.

Where do we get such men as this? Dempsey thought to himself. Then the captain surprised him.

"If I may add something, sir." He looked at Dempsey. "I think we may not be providing our soldiers the best possible training to prepare for this environment."

Dempsey was impressed by the candor. You see, Dempsey was in charge of the entirety of the Army's training, doctrine, and leader development. That meant that each year more than 500,000 soldiers and civilians attended one or more courses under Dempsey's command.

Think about that for a moment—half a million people. During any given three-year period, every single officer, every single rifleman, every tanker and artilleryman, every truck driver, every logistician, statistician, and electrician was trained under Dempsey's watch. It was his responsibility to train people to lead in combat and in humanitarian relief and reconstruction efforts, whether they found themselves in South Asia, the Middle East, Africa, or the Korean Peninsula.

It's important to pause here for a moment and note that the Army excels at training. It provides a host of very realistic scenarios where soldiers practice fighting in simulated wars. On a 198,000-acre installation in Louisiana, the Army runs simulated operations where soldiers jump out of airplanes, try to gain control of a village, and fight in close combat. An entire organization of their fellow soldiers do nothing but train to act as the enemy, and they get very good at it. Hundreds of civilians play the roles of villagers, warring militiamen, NGO staff, and local officials. The simulations and the mock battlefields are so realistic that occasionally people actually die during training.

This brings us back to the fog of war. All of this training, at its core, has to do with the U.S. military's exceptional ability to leverage information.

You want to gather and aggregate as much information as possible to avoid being caught off guard. You want it to be parsed by experts who can piece together a more accurate picture of the operating environment. Moreover, to stay competitive, you want to *guard* the information and prevent it from falling into the enemy's hands. Toward these ends, it makes sense to institute controls.

The same, of course, applies across industries—a pharmaceutical company, for example, guards its research and data tightly to prevent competitors from producing a competing drug or predicting market trends.

Control is best applied within hierarchical organizations, and Dempsey was the head of one very large organization. Here he was, though, being challenged by a twenty-eight-year-old captain for a deficiency in training.

"I've had great training, sir," the captain clarified, almost as if he'd suddenly realized whom he was addressing. "We learned how to fight countries and how to fight organizations," he explained, "but we didn't learn how to fight networks. I've actually just read a book that may interest you. It's titled *The Starfish and the Spider*. Do you know the difference between a starfish and a spider, sir?"

Dempsey had not read the book but, interested in the path on which this young captain was taking him, he said, "Well, to point out the obvious, one lives in the sea and one lives on land. But I don't think that's the distinction you're making."

"If you cut off the head of a spider, it dies. But if you cut off the arm of a starfish, it grows one back."

"Okay. I didn't know that, but I'll take your word for it. So?"

"The important point here, sir, is that the starfish can regenerate because, unlike the spider, the starfish doesn't have a centralized head. It is a decentralized organism. The book I mentioned is pretty persuasive in describing what happens when centralized organizations (spiders) take on decentralized organizations (starfish). Think *Encyclopedia Britannica* versus *Wikipedia*. Think us versus Al Qaeda. You asked what we need. I think we need to figure out how to train the Army to be more starfish-like." The captain went on to explain the book's argument that the harder you fight a starfish, the more distributed— and thus resilient and adaptive—it becomes.

"Thank you, Captain. You've made my trip here today an important one. Well done."

From his multiple tours of duty in Baghdad, Dempsey knew that the most elite of the military's special forces were trained, educated, and equipped for dealing with networks, but he also knew that the captain was correct in pointing out that that knowledge had not been adequately shared and that the institutions of the military had not adequately adapted to this kind of warfare.

A week later, after reading the book, General Dempsey called the author. "Ori, we need to talk," he said, in a conversation that offers us a major clue about exactly what happened in Berkeley and will illuminate a greater force shaping our world.

"I'm about to drive the military toward this adaptation, this evolution I just read about," Dempsey continued. He paused for a moment and added, "I need your help."

Several months later they met in person.

"Have a seat, Ori. Thanks for making the trip here to meet with me."

General Dempsey wasn't sure what would come out of this meeting with Ori Brafman, but he discovered almost immediately that it would be interesting.

Ori sat down in an armchair perpendicular to Dempsey, who sat facing the door.

Ori blew by the pleasantries. Someone had told him that this four-star general's time was very valuable.

"Good to meet you, General. I know you want to talk about my book and about decentralized organizations and networks, but I want to begin by telling you about Burning Man."

"Burning Man?"

"That's right," Ori said, "Burning Man. And about circles."

"Burning Man and circles. Well, I guess if you think it's important to start with Burning Man and circles—whatever that means—then have at it," Dempsey replied. "I've got just a little more than an hour until my next meeting, but I'm eager to learn in the meantime." *And I hope I learn something useful*, Dempsey thought to himself.

Dempsey's executive officer, Colonel Pat White, a highly decorated combat veteran, stood in the doorway listening to this exchange. He was out of Ori's line of sight, but he caught the general's eye and held his hand up to the side of his head, miming a telephone. It was his way of asking Dempsey if he wanted to fake a phone call in order to break off the meeting. The general smiled and shook his head.

It was lunchtime, so Dempsey asked if he could offer Ori something to eat.

"That would be nice," Ori replied, "but you should know that I'm a vegan."

Dempsey leaned back on the couch to take stock of this writer, academic, entrepreneur, vegan. He could sense that Ori was a little bit nervous, speaking far too quickly and leaving everyone behind.

"So, Ori, I feel like I already know almost everything about you, and I'm beginning to wonder if I need to send for a translator to be with us for the rest of the meeting. I can't imagine we have much in common." Then Dempsey laughed. With the tension broken, the meeting began in earnest.

Ninety minutes later the two parted company, but this meeting would be the start of a partnership that is now approaching ten years in the study of leadership.

This inquisitive general and the Berkeley guru.

When you think about it, and granted it isn't obvious, the Army and Burning Man have some interesting things in common. It's not the uniform, although you could argue that both organizations have one (camouflage for the Army, brightly colored fake fur for Burning Man). Nor is it the need to cope in harsh desert environments (admittedly the Nevada desert is likely a far more hospitable place). What unites the two is that both are based on inclusion, but not in the way you'd think.

We often think of inclusion as simply the act of *not excluding*, of not barring anyone. We thus associate inclusion with, basically, letting anyone in the door.

But neither the U.S. Army nor Burning Man is easy to get into. The physical and educational requirements alone render 75% of Americans ineligible to join the Army. While obviously Burning Man attracts a slightly different crowd, making a trek to the Nevada desert also isn't something everyone can do.

The kind of inclusion we're talking about isn't necessarily about admission; it's about participation. In the words of BurningMan.org: "Anyone may be a part of Burning Man. We welcome and respect the stranger. No prerequisites exist for participation in our community."

Think about the Army captain and his desire to effectively participate in helping his country's efforts in Afghanistan. And now consider the people in your organization—they need not be a part of every meeting, but are you enabling them to *participate* in furthering the organization's overall goals?

Personalization: Humanizing the How

Twenty years after having to deal with McVegan, McDonald's has recently had to contend with other detractors. In March of 2017 the company was promoting its special St. Patrick's Day mint Shamrock Shake. In a tweet, the company promoted a ten-second video of a redheaded man wearing a tartan hat and playing bagpipes through milkshake straws. Is it any wonder the company was harshly criticized for using Scottish symbols to promote an Irish holiday?

Could it be, though, that McDonald's got into trouble because it was trying to control the brand? Traditionally, in order to sway public opinion, a company like McDonald's would undertake a strategy built around the old model for building a brand: a carefully structured message designed to reinforce certain attributes. The process is traditionally rather top-down, in the hands of the CEO and other high-level executives.

But any misstep—such as using the wrong cultural reference—is judged as being out of touch.

Maria Sipka's approach with Linquia is to turn things on their head.

Take the example of the Freedom Unlimited credit card, which offered 1.5 percent cash back. Ads touting the benefits of what you could do with the cash you'd be saving were just noise among all the other cards offering various rewards. Consumers don't necessarily want to hear from a bank, and there was no reason to think they were eager to hear about this particular card.

Instead of developing top-down messages, Maria gave influencers $50 and told them to go create an experience.

"Don't just go to a café. Be creative. Have fun. Capture the experience. It's all around, adding a pep in your step," she told them.

That instruction resulted in stories that reminded people to create moments in their day to have some fun. "One was a woman and her boyfriend," Maria recalled. "They grabbed a bottle of wine, went up a hill, and had a great conversation. It's all about the experience that gets created."

Applications for the card skyrocketed because now consumers were receiving a personalized message, one that was tailored to them by people who were part of their community.

From a psychological perspective, this approach might sound like a hard sell for companies. After all, on social media big corporations are favorite targets for criticism, snark, even boycott campaigns. If you're already wary of being criticized when you show your face on social media, why would you want to go even deeper into that hole, surrendering control to strangers and not even knowing who will be creating stories about your product?

Reflects Maria, "When you're a brand and your media is highly centralized on your social channels and on your website where you invite people to engage, you're going to have a flood of haters, all the detractors, who are going to try to annihilate you in every shape and form. That's a given."

Thus when McDonald's turned to Linquia, you can imagine the apprehension the company's executives must have felt: What will the influencers say? And how much trouble will those messages get us into?

However, something surprising happened. When McDonald's activated grassroots influencers and decentralized the promotion of the Shamrock Shake, only 1 percent of influencer-generated messages garnered negative comments. The explanation? A corporation is an easy target that everybody loves to hate. But who wants to criticize a flesh-and-blood person telling a human story?

Reflected Pollack: "What got me really excited is the democratization of content. Social platforms created ways to connect, which is the new age of media, having multitude points of contact rather than a single-channel broadcast. I never thought that people's natural social connections, audiences, and communities could be used to channel a brand: in the way that anyone with a room could be an Airbnb host, and anyone with a car can be an Uber driver, anyone who is a community leader can be an advertisement channel for a brand."

Linquia's micro-influencers are stay-at-home moms, retirees, students—not the kinds of people who'd typically be working at, say, an advertising agency. But they do have the time to develop content and are pleased to be included in the conversation. And as members of the communities they are trying to reach, they are much more likely than advertising agencies to come up with messages that are emotionally salient.

Whether you're communicating with customers or managing employees, you can rely on inclusion to humanize your message and deliver it more effectively.

Inclusion is about concentrating the *what* (i.e., the directive, the goal) and distributing the *how*. After meeting the young captain in Afghanistan and speaking with the Berkeley guru in his office, Dempsey introduced into army training and education a concept called Mission Command: tell your subordinates what you want accomplished, and loosen control to allow them to develop strategies to achieve the desired outcome.

Purpose: Bringing the Cause to the Community

Traditional efforts to mobilize groups of people follow the assumption that once you've identified a worthy cause (whatever it may be), you must then build a community around it. The problem with this approach is that it's hugely time consuming, and every new cause requires a new supporting community to be built from the ground up.

But what if we flip this notion and bring a cause to a pre-existing community? Then the cause becomes the *what* and the community, already vibrant and thriving, rallies around to determine the *how*.

"As a business," explains Maria, "you need to have an ideology, and you need to inspire and inform your audience. You have to let go of the way the message is crafted, and you need to trust these group leaders who have opted in and who are going to go and tell the story."

What are the preexisting communities that exist within your organization? How can you harness their power by giving them a purpose aligned with the organizational goals? And who are the influencers within these communities whose impact you can tap?

"Audiences are much more diverse than you may expect," Maria explained. "Maybe they all love nature photography, but they have such a large demographic distribution that traditional targeting isn't even effective."

In other words, the people following a leader within a community may have a very wide variance among them, so you'd be hard pressed to find a traditional channel that would effectively reach that whole population.

Reflects Maria, "The definition of a community leader is broadening. Anyone could be an influencer. If you're passionate about something and other people are passionate about it, and you have the discipline to post regularly, then you have what it takes."

CHAPTER 4: **THE COST OF CONTROL**

The Element of Surprise

"It's pretty incredible," Colin Hoy, a PhD candidate in neuroscience, said of the brain, "that there's a couple of pounds of liquid squishy stuff that controls everything about us."

As it turns out, our very own brain serves as an excellent model for understanding organizational behavior and the challenges of inclusive leadership.

Like a leader interested in learning exactly what's going on within their organization, scientists are curious about what's really going on inside the human brain, and have been since we learned that the brain serves as the body's metaphorical CEO.

But how do you gain access to what's going on in the brain to learn about how it operates? In attempting to answer this question, neurologists face two major challenges, one having to do with time and the other with space.

In the 1920s neuropsychologists gained information about the brain using the electroencephalogram (EEG)—attaching electrodes to the scalp to pick up brain waves. In so doing, they were able to detect exactly when an electric current was discharged.

This is very useful information, but it's a little bit like pressing a cup against a wall to listen in on a party next door: you'd know exactly when someone spoke, but you'd be in the dark about where in the neighboring room they were standing.

The converse is true of functional magnetic resonance imaging (fMRI), which uses magnetism to measure blood flow in the various parts of the brain. An fMRI provides a 3D image of blood flow, showing which brain regions get activated in response to a prompt.

But as with the EEG, there's a catch: because the flow of blood is much slower than the firing of neurons, an fMRI can't show how the brain operates in real time. It can only tell us what brain areas might be involved in a given task.

The holy grail for brain researchers has been to place electrodes right inside the brain. That would allow them to know both *where* a signal originated and also precisely *when* it was generated.

But to conduct such a measurement, neuroscientists would have to find subjects willing to, well, have electrodes placed inside their heads. And even if they were able to recruit volunteers, the invasive surgery required to implant electrodes would carry a nontrivial risk of permanent brain damage. Ethics boards would never allow it.

Fortunately, there's a clever solution that is providing exactly what researchers have been hoping for.

Accompanied by a neurosurgeon, Hoy enters what appears to be a typical hospital room, with a bed, a couple of chairs, and a few family visiting members.

Occasionally a member of the hospital staff enters the room to monitor vital signs and any changes in the patient's condition. But the patient is wearing something you wouldn't normally see in a hospital room: what at first looks like a large turban.

On closer inspection, it becomes clear that there are wires protruding from the headpiece, and those wires are connected to a nearby machine. Hoy, armed with a stack of legal paper-work, asks the patient whether she's still willing to participate in the study. She agrees, and Hoy begins his work.

The young woman suffers from epilepsy, and her seizures have been so frequent and troubling that the doctors have decided the risks of surgery are worth the potential benefits of understanding where the seizures are generated and, in turn, what can be done to stop them.

The patient is recovering from an operation that took place just yesterday to place electrodes in her brain—not for pur-poses of Hoy's laboratory or research but to treat her epilepsy. Cases like this provide Hoy access to individuals with electrodes *already* placed inside their brains.

Weighing the risks to the patients and the benefits to sci-ence as a whole, ethical boards have granted neuropsychologists access to these epilepsy patients, provided that they adhere to certain rules and limitations.

Neuropsychologists began by asking the patients to solve puzzles or complete other gamelike tasks. This allowed them to isolate precisely which parts of the brain are activated when we make a given type of decision.

Over time, they noticed that whenever a participant made a mistake, an immediate electrical signal appeared. "We're talking about a tenth of a second after the error was committed," explained Hoy. That means that before we even have time to consciously real-ize that we've made a mistake, let alone consider its ramifications, our brain has already gone on high alert.

Neuroscientists soon realized that the error signals weren't really associated with mistakes per se, but more generally with *surprises*: whenever reality failed to match the patient's expecta-tion, the signal would go off.

Have you ever had that awkward sensation of putting your foot forward to walk down a step, but in reality there's no step there? Your foot falls awkwardly on the flat surface as your balance readjusts and you realize you anticipated a step where none was. Or how about reaching for a glass of wine while looking the other way, but grasping nothing because someone has moved the glass? In both instances the error signal would fire in your brain.

Looking into the matter further, neuroscientists discovered that these error signals are generated by specific parts of the brain that are dedicated to noticing anomalies. Let's call these regions "surprise neurons." Rather than sift through the massive amount of data coming in about what's going on around you, considering each piece and what it means, your brain simply goes about its business, relying on the surprise neurons to raise the alarm when something unexpected happens. It's a very efficient approach.

And your brain reacts sharply to surprises. When something happens that catches you off guard, you immediately course-correct and almost instantly shift your core assumptions to better navigate the environment.

Now, what works for the brain also works for organizations. They just need to identify and engage their own "surprise neurons."

If the Glove Doesn't Fit

The Albert Einstein Medical Center in Philadelphia is representative of many large businesses—it has a vast patient pool, a limited budget, and various units that can't always communicate with one another.

For years the hospital, like many others around the country, has been plagued by a germ that is responsible for more yearly deaths in the United States than HIV/AIDS. Antibiotic-resistant staph infection (MRSA) has been on a steady rise—and your best bet for picking it up is to spend time in a hospital. But unlike other deadly germs, MRSA spreads in a way that's completely preventable. We've known exactly how to avoid it since the late 1800s: health professionals need only wash their hands before seeing each patient and consistently wear protective gloves and gowns.

There are a million reasons, though, why even the best doctors fail to gown up. It's not that they don't recognize the importance of being safe; small factors just get in the way.

The Albert Einstein Center, seeing rising rates of preventable patient deaths due to MRSA, decided to take action.

Rather than just printing informational pamphlets about the importance of hygienic practices, the hospital's head of infection control assembled a selection of staff members representative of all levels and all roles, from surgeons to janitors.

During the session, a man named Jasper—a high school dropout and Vietnam veteran whose job was to transport patients between rooms and to empty the trash—raised his hand. The astute observation he was about to make would become a literal life-saver.

"I've noticed," he began, "that in the wing with a lot of MRSA infections, the garbage cans are always nearly empty. They don't have any gloves in them."

Trying to solve the riddle of what was going on, the group went to that unit and asked the nurses why they weren't using gloves.

It turned out that the nurses in that particular wing all happened to have very small hands. But because the hospital stocked equal numbers of each glove size, the extra-small gloves would always run out before the rest. Larger sizes were cumbersome and made simple tasks awkward and difficult, so the nurses were often going without.

"Would you wear gloves if we stocked more extra-smalls?" asked the head of infection control.

"Of course we would!" replied the nurses.

Jasper then took out a Sharpie and wrote down his phone number, so that every time the unit ran low on extra-small gloves, they could simply pick up the phone, and within minutes Jasper would provide a refill.

It was incremental change like this that lowered patient mortality by 70 percent in one year.

Now, this is not to say that the whole hospital should have been stocked with more extra-small gloves. Nor should the janitor have been promoted to head of infection control.

Rather, using the neuron analogy, the janitor in this case happened to be the key "surprise neuron"—the one guy who saw the garbage bags with enough frequency that he was able to notice the anomaly. A surgeon might have passed the garbage cans dozens of times without ever picking up on the anomaly. And including him in the conversation allowed the "brain" (hospital administration) to receive his message.

We can use such organizational "neurons" to avoid the pitfalls of bad intel within our organizations. We need to have as many Jaspers around us as possible—people who will notice and be surprised by different things than we will. And we need to delegate to them the task of being surprised.

Reflect for a moment about the kinds of processes and procedures that organizations utilize to prevent surprises. Vast amounts of money are spent to ensure that managers get even the most minute details. But a manager sifting through a mountain of information may not be very well positioned to notice small but crucial anomalies.

Virtually no company has in place a dragnet similar to that of the human brain to pick up on surprises in various levels and corners of the organization. But imagine for a moment you're the CEO of a large organization, and you're able to learn about anything unusual right when it happens—not by sifting through all the facts yourself, but by surrounding yourself with the right people and making sure the anomalies they notice get conveyed to you.

You would have the opportunity to address each surprise with intention and change the company's course of action to better navigate the business environment. Think about how much more effective you would be than the CEO of your competitor, who may have all the facts at his fingertips but rarely learns about the surprises occurring within his organization. Can organizations create a process akin to our brain's response to surprise?

Overcome the Ace

Unfortunately, it's not sufficient to merely surround ourselves with as many organizational surprise neurons as possible. We need to create both mechanisms to encourage them to sound the surprise alarm and systems to attune ourselves to the signal when it comes.

In the workshops he runs, Ori often does an exercise in which each participant randomly picks from a shuffled deck of playing cards but isn't allowed to look at which card they drew.

Once everyone has a card in hand, Ori counts to three, and they all lift their respective cards to their foreheads—so you can see everyone else's card, and everyone can see yours, but you don't know what card *you* hold.

He next tells the participants to pretend they're at a company picnic where the ace represents the CEO, the king is the VP, and so on, down to the twos, which are the lowest. The task is for everyone to interact with one another giving clues as to the other person's standing in the fictional company. Over the years, he's heard people give heavy-handed clues—"Hey, are you staying at the Motel . . . 6?" (nudge, nudge, wink, wink)—so now he cautions them against being too obvious. He's also had senior leaders—people who're in charge of thousands of people—intentionally walk by mirrors so that they can sneak a peek at the cards on their foreheads, so he's had to start covering up mirrors during the exercise. Apparently, we all want to know where we stand.

As they mill around, Ori reminds the participants to keep meeting other people. After a few minutes of this, he asks them to line up—without talking or looking at their cards—in rank order. Without fail, the group nails it.

The threes line up ahead of the twos, the jacks right above the tens but below the queens. You'd think military folks, accustomed to a rigid rank system, would be exceptional at this task. But CEOs are just as good at it. So are nonprofit managers, social activists, and UC Berkeley students.

Still, when he tells participants they can finally look at their cards, they're surprised by how quickly they each knew their place on the ladder. No matter our age, profession, or industry, as humans we're highly sensitive to status.

"What was your first hint that you were a two?" Ori asked a manager recently.

"Well, for starters, no one looked at me. No one came to talk to me. And the people who did come and say hi told me to 'keep doing a good job.'"

Conversely, every single time Ori runs the exercise, the ace knows his or her status right away. People call the ace "sir" or "ma'am." They don't interrupt when the ace is speaking. They laugh at the ace's stupid jokes.

When Ori ran the exercise in his undergraduate business class, sure enough, the students knew exactly where they stood in the arbitrary made-up social ladder.

In this specific instance, two of the most popular women in the class—smart, motivated, bright, friendly—drew twos. They stood chatting in one corner as the ace entertained the king and queen in another corner.

"Did the ace ever come up to you?" Ori asked the twos. Of course not.

"Did you ever go up to the ace?"

"No," said one of the twos.

"But it's not like you were shy—I saw you walking up to another two. What were you talking about?"

Without missing a beat, she responded, "We were talking about how this party sucked."

Now, it's easy to understand why the twos weren't having a good time. Who wants to be at the bottom of the totem pole? And it's equally easy to understand why they wouldn't be going over to announce their displeasure to the ace. But here's what is really fairly shocking.

When Ori asked the ace what he'd been talking about with his fellow royalty, he said, "We were chatting about how *fun* this [made-up, remember] picnic was!" The ace had no idea that the twos weren't having a good time.

From a two's perspective, every incentive is to keep quiet. You don't want to alienate the ace—at best, maybe you'll be patronized, and who wants that?

If you're an ace, no one below you is going to tell you that there's a problem. You can be the nicest, friendliest person, but because you have an ace on your forehead, everyone else's incentive is to *lie* to you.

How many times have you met a leader who thinks they're beloved by their people, but you then speak to their direct reports and learn that the initiatives put forth by the leader are a complete mess? It's not that these leaders are out of touch; it's just that they are blinded by being the ace.

In the chapters to come, we look at specific tools, leadership principles and instincts, that actually foster inclusion. This isn't a philosophy; it's an ongoing practice to stay attuned to the knowledge that so easily gets withheld or ignored.

CHAPTER 5: **THE POWER OF BELONGING**

Historical Roots

Since the 1940s a sense of belonging has been recognized as a human psychological need and one of the major sources for human motivation. It's important to us; whether we're conscious of it or not, a sense of belonging keeps us healthy and happy.

Belongingness developed to serve an evolutionary need: those who formed mutual attachments to others enjoyed the safety of numbers and were less likely to wander off alone into danger. Anthropologists have suggested that it was humans' ability to form and comprehend more complex vocal sounds— the rudiments of language and the foundation of our identity as a social species—that enabled us to survive, ultimately outlasting our hominid neighbors like the Neanderthals, Denisovans, and *Homo floresiensis*.[4] As social beings, we protected one another, shared resources, and collaborated to gain advantages over other species.

---

4. *Mitch Prinstein, "Popular People Live Longer," New York Times, June 1, 2017.*

Though deeply rooted in basic survival in a very different world, the need to belong hasn't faded over time. Today and millennia ago, belongingness consists of the combination of a sense of identity (how we distinguish ourselves from others), a sense of security (the opposite of powerlessness), and a sense of order (structure and predictability).

"Belonging" can be a pretty vague term. That is, we all know what it means to belong to something, but it's hard to distinguish levels of belonging. What does it actually mean to be included?

You may be a member of an airline's frequent flyer program, so in a sense you belong. But that level of belonging is much less significant than, say, being a member of a church or of a team at work. Theoretically, we could ask individuals how "much" belonging they feel toward an organization or a cause—but doing so would at best yield approximate, qualitative data.

Thus, for our purposes here, let's set a high bar for what we mean by "belonging." The highest such bar is being willing to set aside your individual interests in order to advance the interests of the group.

Think of a mother, for example, willing to go hungry so her kids can eat; think of a soldier who risks his or her life for comrades and country. Psychologically, we do so not just out of altruism but because of a belief that by advancing the cause of the group, we advance our own narrative.

As humans, belonging to a family unit ensures our survival—our family members' willingness to sacrifice for us should we need their help provides us security and safety.

There are multiple reasons why people may feel connected. We see these as:

1. Feeling that your efforts on behalf of the group are meaningful

2. Being able to imagine how your contribution will have a meaningful impact
3. Receiving rapid feedback about the impact you've had
4. Having positive memories associated with belonging
5. Feeling invited to belong, as opposed to ordered
6. Engaging within a context whereby you are part of the overall group narrative

The development of industrial society raised fears that we were losing our sense of community—that the faceless, anonymous sprawl of the world's cities was depriving us of the basic ability to feel as though we are part of something bigger than ourselves. And in the 1980s researchers began studying belonging and have unequivocally come to the realization that it is, in fact, a need: without it, humans suffer both mentally and physically.

The Science Behind It

In an effort to understand how we experience belonging and exclusion, some researchers have focused on the anterior angulate cortex, or ACC, the part of the brain that becomes active when we experience physical pain.

One study aimed to find out if the ACC would become active when individuals experienced rejection.[5] fMRI images were captured while participants played a virtual ball-tossing game with two other players. They were told that the other players were fellow study participants, also in fMRI machines. In actuality, the other "players" were part of a computer program.

---

5. *Naomi I. Eisenberger, Matthew D. Lieberman, and Kipling D. Williams, "Does Rejection Hurt? An fMRI Study of Social Exclusion,"* Science 302, no. 5643 (October 10, 2003): 290–92.

At the beginning of the game, participants were told that due to technical difficulties, the links to the other players' machines couldn't be made, so the participant would have to watch the other two play before joining in. Researchers observed that when test subjects were arbitrarily left out of the game, the ACC did in fact become active. The results of the study suggest that the feeling of rejection has a similar effect on the human brain to that of physical pain.

Social exclusion can also hinder our thinking and cognitive processes. In one study, participants scored significantly lower on IQ tests and other cognitive tasks after experiencing rejection; even just being told that they were likely to end up alone in life, or be socially excluded at the time of their death, affected their ability to process and act intelligently.[6]

So what happens when people actually do live lonely lives?

In a meta-analysis of 148 studies with a total of over 308,000 participants aged between six and ninety-two from all over the world, psychologist Julianne Holt-Lunstad of Brigham Young University made a surprising discovery: the size of a person's network, their number of friends, whether they live alone, and whether they participate in social activities are predictive of that person's life span.[7] People with larger networks, who have good-quality relationships, have a remarkably increased chance of survival over time. In fact, the results of the analysis demonstrate that social exclusion is more harmful to us than obesity, physical inactivity, and binge drinking.

The only comparable health hazard? Smoking.

Low social connectedness not only is a predictor of natural life expectancy but also is a significant predictor of suicide

---

6. *Roy F. Baumeister, Jean M. Twenge, and Christopher K. Nuss, "Effects of Social Exclusion on Cognitive Processes: Anticipated Aloneness Reduces Intelligent Thought,"* Journal of Personality and Social Psychology 83, no. 4 (2002): 817–27.

7. *Julianne Holt-Lunstad, Timothy B. Smith, and J. Bradley Layton, "Social Relationships and Mortality Risk: A Meta-analytic Review,"* PLOS Medicine 7, no. 7 (July 27, 2010): e1000316.

attempt.[8] A 1994 study on social integration demonstrated a near-perfect correlation between family growth activity (marriage, lack of divorce, birth rates) and homicide rates.[9]

What is the link between a lack of connections and self-destructive or violent behavior?

When we experience social exclusion, we perceive our lives as less meaningful.[10] Being excluded by our families, close friends, and romantic partners has the greatest effect.[11] And just as social exclusion is correlated with a less meaningful life, a sense of belonging is strongly positively correlated with perceived meaningfulness of life. This is true across age groups.[12] But when compared with older adults, those aged eighteen to twenty-four report feeling very differently from adults in other age groups in terms of their relationship to belongingness. In a 2007 comprehensive study conducted in the United Kingdom, this youngest group of adults reported feeling they didn't belong to any one group, and that they believed their sense of belonging would not always be rooted in the same people, places, and beliefs.[13] This stands in contrast to their older counterparts, who reported feeling a sense of belonging to a single group that was less likely to change.

Those in the eighteen-to-twenty-four-year-old age group were more likely to feel that their sense of belonging came from

---

8. Tohru Takizawa et al., "Stress Buffering Effects of Social Support on Depressive Symptoms in Middle Age: Reciprocity and Community Mental Health," Psychiatry and Clinical Neurosciences 60, no. 6 (December 2006): 652–61.

9. Jean M. Twenge et al., "If You Can't Join Them, Beat Them: Effects of Social Exclusion on Aggressive Behavior," Journal of Personality and Social Psychology 81, no. 6 (2001): 1058–69.

10. Tyler F. Stillman et al., "Alone and Without Purpose: Life Loses Meaning Following Social Exclusion," Journal of Experimental Social Psychology 45, no. 4 (July 2009): 686–94.

11. Twenge et al., "If You Can't Join Them, Beat Them."

12. Nathanial M. Lambert et al., "To Belong Is to Matter: Sense of Belonging Enhances Meaning in Life," Personality and Social Psychology Bulletin 39, no. 11 (2013): 1418–27.

13. Social Issues Research Centre, "Belonging" (research commissioned by the Automobile Association, July 2007), www.sirc.org/publik/belonging.pdf.

a wide variety and number of groups that was constantly changing. In the workplace, they found it nearly twice as easy to leave their jobs as those over twenty-four.

Have young people always felt this way about belongingness, as a result of factors related to age or life stage, or has the landscape of belongingness changed, altering the experience of social belongingness for this group?

We argue that though people may feel more rooted the older they get, the change in the social fabric of today's society has made belongingness a little more complicated, especially for young people, whose experience is dominated by the digital world.

The New Context

In the past our sense of belonging was rigidly defined in terms of traditional markers of social identity: our families, close friendships, lifestyle choices, nationalities, professional identities, and hobbies. Think back to the predigitized era, when our network connections were limited to those in our immediate geographic areas, at best stretched to include the occasional pen pal. Today, for the first time in human history, via the Internet, people are able to create their own geographically dispersed belonging categories.

We can seek and find groups whose members could be anywhere across the globe. And the complexity and size of these new networks give what is now labeled "globalization" a peculiar force in influencing belonging.

The world of social networks, from the vast to the niche, has become ubiquitous in our lives. They exist not only in addition to our jobs, our personal lives, and our hobbies and communities, but also as a medium through which we participate in our workplaces, our friendship circles, and our geographical communities.

Social networks have broken down communication barriers by simplifying the exchange of information among friends, coworkers, and strangers alike, thus allowing culture to spread and influence the information around us. Not only are those members who are born into a culture able to be a part of it, but outsiders who are interested in it can also learn about it, join it, and celebrate it.

Social media networks are now markers of our social identities, a part of everything we do, and they are giving us power we've never before experienced.

Though mass media has always had the ability to shape public opinion, the Internet has put this power into the hands of every user. Simply by participating in a social media network, an individual has the ability to start a movement, become a leader, and gain a following.

YouTube is now the world's largest mass communication medium, allowing each and every person to create content and spread a message across the world. Social networking sites like YouTube empower us to learn, to participate, to lead, and to follow groups and communities we may never before have been able to connect with.

Where we once had barriers to engaging with individuals and groups all over the world, these walls no longer exist. We can start groups and seek them out in order to be included—no matter where, no matter when.

Facebook and Twitter are no strangers to the idea that social networking sites have a place in the world of belongingness; in fact, they emphasize that achieving a sense of belonging comes from engaging in the ongoing, real-time flow of digital self-expression. Facebook urges you to "connect with friends and the world around you" by participating in your personal news feed. Twitter tells you to "find out what's happening right now, with the people and organizations you care about."

The positive messaging holds up. Studies have demonstrated that the Internet environment is very supportive of friendships, romances, volunteerism, fund-raising, and every variety of support group an individual might seek out. In fact, the Internet is particularly welcoming to certain kinds of support groups: those whose members feel stigmatized by society and are reluctant to share their concerns with their "home" networks through personal and public discourse.

A well-known example of a stigmatized group finding support and strength in numbers via the Internet is the "It Gets Better" project launched by Dan Savage and Terry Miller in 2010 in response to rising suicide rates among LGBT teens. A video created by Savage and Miller went viral, and more than fifty thousand more videos like it, from people of all races and creeds across the world, were added to the movement.

But it has long been argued that while the Internet, along with the mobile devices we carry to access it, offers perpetual human contact and access to groups worldwide, it's conducive, ironically, to independent mobility, fleeting social connections, and self-promotion.

Prompts in your Facebook newsfeed ("How are you feeling?"), emojis that share your mood with one click, and suggestions to add posts about life events promote a hyperpreoccupation with the self. The sheer variety of tools available to us to broadcast our personal information suggests we should consume ourselves and our network connections with this information.

But as you broadcast your personal information, are you truly being heard? Is there a real connection, and do you really belong to a mutual group? Even if you do feel a sense of belonging to that group online, are you likely to feel and behave as you would if the group existed in the "real world"? The short answer is no. Research has shown that the predictable ways in which we operate as individuals in groups play out entirely differently online.[14] Researchers have been surprised by how quickly and easily people become disinhibited when socializing online versus in a real-life context. When compared with traditional group behavior, people engage in aversive social behavior in the digital world extremely easily.

Aversive social behavior in the group setting is puzzling. These kinds of behaviors threaten a person's belongingness to a group—who wants to hang out with the bully? But aversive social behaviors are sometimes performed in order to amplify belongingness. People engage in these behaviors in order to influence and control others. The result in many cases is that the individual feels empowered or energized.

But why does this happen so much more easily and frequently in the digital context? Researchers argue that due to the "invisible" nature of online interactions, there is less incentive to act in socially appropriate ways.[15] Imagine that a selection of fifty dog owners from across the United States are all put together in one room with instructions to remain silent and still. If we were tasked with entering the room and writing down every bit of information we could about this group in one minute, what might we jot down?

Well, we would likely first mention the piece of information we've already been given: that everyone in the room owns a dog. Next we could determine a number of other pieces of information through basic observation, such as that the group includes both men and women. We might see a wide range in age, from a high school student to a grayed retiree. We could point out that there are individuals of different races, different heights, different hair colors, and different sizes. We might notice that some are fashionable, some have facial hair, some wear glasses, and some are physically disabled.

14. Patricia Wallace, The Psychology of the Internet, 2nd ed. (New York: Cambridge University Press, 2016).

15. Social Issues Research Centre, "Belonging."

In a short amount of time, we would be able to draw a lot of information about the personal characteristics of the members of the group without their speaking or communicating in any way.

But let's take that same group, leave them in their homes in front of their computers, and put them in an online forum. When we enter the forum, all we see is a list of usernames, and possibly a small photo selected by each individual that may or may not include the person's face, body, or self in any way. Now what can we write down about them?

Our list would likely be shortened to just a couple of facts: that they are all dog owners and perhaps that the group is of mixed gender. Personal characteristics would be virtually absent.

SIDE (Social Identity Model of Deindividuation Effects) theory explains what happens when personal characteristics are obscured or invisible, as they are in anonymous online groups. Rather than focus on the characteristics of the individual, members of the group double down on a common social identity. Research suggests that in online groups, individuals feel stronger attachment to the group's identity than to their own personal identities; in fact, personal identity is all but erased due to the lack of nonverbal cues highlighting individual differences.[16]

This makes for an extremely cohesive in-group: one that suppresses individuality and magnifies the differences between the in-group and outsiders. There are obvious implications for online communities espousing extremist views of any stripe.

So while Facebook and Twitter are driving users to focus on their individual experience online, that experience is becoming more and more about the groups to which the individual belongs.

What can we do as leaders for our teams and their personal senses of belonging? Why should we care?

The human desire to belong holds a key to understanding how to lead in our current environment. As we discover a sense

---

16. *Wallace,* Psychology of the Internet, *pp. 20–21.*

of belonging to a team, organization, cause, or community, we find that our goals are in line with those of the group and with those of the leaders and other members of our team. With our combined efforts aligned and everyone working toward a common goal, we find a sense of control that produces a sense of order for each of us within the organization, and this trickles into our individual daily lives.

Where we have order, we have predictability—predictability in our actions and the actions of those around us. It is this predictability that allows leaders to take the actions necessary to build and uphold the vision of the organization.

Feeling that we matter to our organization and are safe within it reaffirms and strengthens our sense of belonging. When people feel they belong, they engage more and are more productive. Belonging helps us achieve understanding, and the feeling that we understand those around us, and that they understand us, strengthens the positive bonds among the members of the team and its leaders and enhances our feelings of self-worth.

Belonging has relevance not only for individual well-being but also for the organization. By bringing the right people into a meeting, task, or job at the right time for a particular purpose, you can build a sense of individual purpose while successfully utilizing your resources to achieve your goals. Belonging also serves leaders in their mission to establish a sense of positive conformity within the organization. When we belong, we tend to adopt the attitudes and behaviors of those around us.

When people lack a sense of belonging, they instinctively seek it in unhealthy ways that may be destructive to your organization.

In short, a lack of belonging within an organization not only results in negativity and ineffectiveness but also opens the door for team members to find the sense of belonging they so desperately need in competing or unhealthy causes, which can be damaging to individuals and catastrophic for organizations.

In the new environment, the true sense of belonging we used to gain from our communities isn't as prevalent. For some it may not exist at all. Simultaneously, endless pathways to belonging are available to us via technology, social media, and the ubiquitous flow of information they offer.

In a world where people are not readily feeling as if they belong to a positive cause, and where everyone has the ability to belong to something, we need to help our team members make good decisions regarding the efforts with which they choose to identify.

If leaders fail to provide this for their subordinates, these people will find belonging for themselves in ways that will be decidedly unhelpful in our effort to produce order and shape the outcomes of our actions.

As the sense of true belonging seems to erode around us, we as leaders must create real and authentic ways for our subordinates to feel that they are a part of something meaningful. We must create environments wherein individuals feel they are the "first among equals." As leaders, we must commit a certain amount of every day, every month, and every year to ensuring that people feel a sense of belonging in our organizations.

PART 3

THE INCLUSIVE LEADER

CHAPTER 6: **BELONGING ISN'T OPTIONAL**

Leadership Principle #1: Give Them Memories

Leaders are busy. Most would say that they have more to do and less time to do it than ever before. It's probably true. After all, leaders still have to do the things they have always been expected to do, but with the added challenge of managing exponentially more information and competing with digital echoes for the attention, trust, and confidence of their followers.

Leaders have always had to compete for the trust and confidence of their followers. However, that competition has become more intense—and more important—in the era of digital echoes. It's actually pretty simple. If people don't feel like they belong to your group, department, company, or corporation, they easily can and probably will find something else to believe in and belong to.

The most important responsibility of leaders—no matter how busy they are and how many other priorities demand their attention—is to make their people feel like they belong.

Opportunities to make our followers feel they belong are all around us, opportunities to "give them memories" so that they know we care about them by investing in them our scarcest resource: time.

Leaders have to develop an instinct for communicating a sense of belonging to their followers and then be alert for opportunities to do so. A private word in the hallway. A compliment at a meeting. The willingness to listen for just a few minutes beyond our usual attention span. The habit of explaining in a constructive way how some paper, proposal, or briefing could have been done better. Beginning conversations with an inquiry about the well-being of the person or their family. A handwritten note to express condolences, congratulations, or appreciation. An unexpected phone call or unannounced visit.

Producing memories of success, memories of failure, reinforcing a feeling of commitment and belonging.

Give them memories, or someone else will.

• • •

It was 1975, and young Lieutenant Dempsey, officer-in-charge of a remote German outpost five miles from the Iron Curtain, wasn't fond of surprises. There was an ever-present fear that an escalation in conflict might suddenly take the "cold" out of the Cold War. If the Soviets decided to invade West Germany through Czechoslovakia, this small military installation was the first line of defense.

The camp looked exactly how you would picture a frontline military base in the middle of a German forest. The eight-hundred-yard-square perimeter was surrounded by chain-link fence topped with barbed wire. Six metal Quonset huts served as administrative offices and living quarters.

When a sergeant approached Dempsey to let him know there was an unannounced guest at the gate, Dempsey's radar went up. Such a surprise, he knew, could mean trouble.

As it turned out, this was a very unusual sort of surprise. Waiting at the perimeter of the base, the sergeant told him, was not an enemy but a nun.

"What did you say, Sergeant?" Dempsey wanted to make sure he'd heard correctly.

"A nun, sir."

Dempsey was curious; he wanted to ask the sergeant how a nun had made it to the remote base when the nearest village was more than ten miles away. But his practical side prevailed. He was monitoring a patrol maneuvering along the border, and he didn't want to be distracted.

"Tell her I'm really busy. Ask her to come back another time."

Five minutes later, the sergeant was back. The nun was not going to leave until she got to talk to Dempsey. *Maybe it really is a nun,* he thought, recalling the persistence of the nuns who had taught him in grammar school in Bayonne, New Jersey.

Out of some combination of curiosity and caution—what would his mother say if he disrespected a nun?—Dempsey decided to make an appearance. Sure enough, standing at the gate was a petite elderly woman dressed in a black habit. She eagerly greeted Dempsey.

She confidently introduced herself. "Hello, Lieutenant, I'm Sister Mary Cecilia. I'm from Milwaukee but recently arrived over here as part of a mission in Konnersreuth," she said, naming a small German village about ten kilometers away. "One of the other sisters in the convent told me about this small group of Americans in the middle of the forest. I've come to pray with your soldiers. Today is Sunday, you know." She said it in the same casual way that housekeeping personnel at a hotel announce through your door that they've come to clean your room.

Caught off guard and unaccustomed to taking orders from those in any uniform other than that of the U.S. Army—at least since grammar school—Dempsey politely turned her away. She agreed to leave, declining the offer of a ride back to the convent, but only after noting that she would be back for another visit on a future Sunday and expected Dempsey to allow her into the camp.

Sure enough, exactly two weeks later, the nun once again appeared at the base. This time, though, having gained some assurances that she was in fact who she said she was, Dempsey allowed her to enter. Without missing a beat, she walked briskly toward the basketball court, where a group of Dempsey's most unruly and least disciplined soldiers were in the midst of an intense game.

"Where are you going?" Dempsey hurried along behind her, trying to avert an impending disaster. He could only imagine the soldiers' reaction to a nun interfering with their game.

"I'm going over to that group of soldiers right there," Sister Mary Cecilia announced nonchalantly.

"Sister," Dempsey said with a note of caution, "that particular group of soldiers can be kind of rough, and they're not going to appreciate you interrupting their game."

Dempsey wasn't exaggerating. This particular group of men were disgruntled draftees from a very difficult period in the Army's history, including several who were awaiting judicial punishment and discharge for charges involving drugs, racism, and violence.

Imagine the look on these tough soldiers' faces when, right in the middle of the game, a nun appeared out of nowhere and announced, "I'm here to pray with you, young men." The scene was so surreal that they didn't know how to react. They glanced at each other with a mix of confusion and impatience, looking for cues about how to respond, then looked at Dempsey contemptuously, as if to say, "I can't believe you brought her here."

Of course, the basketball players had no way of knowing that Dempsey was just as perplexed by the nun as they were. But now he faced a dilemma. He could throw the nun under the bus, shrug his shoulders, and allow the soldiers to continue their game, or he could defend the nun and absorb the anger that would be directed his way. Dempsey took the middle ground, introducing the nun and telling the men they could pray with her if they wished, but assuring them that it was their choice.

Whether they were caught off guard or there was some divine intervention, the men stopped their game and prayed with the nun. After the brief prayer she asked them about themselves and their families. The soldiers were warm and open, each sharing his story, feeling that the nun genuinely wanted to know about them. After her time with the group on the basketball court, she made the rounds of the camp, meeting with groups of soldiers until dark. At the end of the day, as Dempsey was seeing her off—this time she accepted the offer of a ride—the nun had one more surprise in store for him. She had a question.

"Why didn't you want me to talk to those soldiers at the basketball court earlier today?" She wasn't afraid to be straight-forward.

Dempsey answered her diplomatically. "A few of them aren't my best soldiers."

"But they're still your soldiers, right?" she countered, not really caring that she might be upsetting her host.

"Yes, of course. Why do you ask?" Dempsey tried not to sound defensive.

"Well, have you given up on them?"

"Of course not!" he objected, realizing immediately that the nun might have picked up on something he had missed. Perhaps he had lost a *bit* of faith in *some* of his soldiers.

"That's good," she reflected. "You should never give up on people."

Dempsey bid Sister Mary Cecilia farewell and immersed himself in deep thought. Had he really lost faith in some of his followers?

From that day forward he resolved never to give up on his soldiers. If they had the courage to commit to serving their country, Dempsey would match their service and commitment by serving them. Over the years there were soldiers who gave up on the army and failed to embrace the military ethos, and they had to go. But Dempsey would not be the first one to quit. He would make sure each soldier under his influence felt that he or she was part of the team, that he or she belonged.

Years later, in 1998, as Colonel Dempsey was giving up command of the Third Armored Cavalry Regiment at Fort Carson, a tall, thin master sergeant—the second-highest enlisted rank in the Army—came through the receiving line to congratulate him.

"Hello, sir. Do you remember me?"

Dempsey remembered his face but couldn't remember where they had served together in what was at that point his twenty-fourth year of military service.

"I'm Greg Vincent from back in the Second Cavalry in 1975. You were my platoon leader."

Greg Vincent. One of the soldiers on the basketball court when Sister Mary Cecilia made her appearance at the border camp.

"Hello, Master Sergeant! I see you've done quite well for yourself. Congratulations."

"You too, sir. And thanks for giving me a second chance. I know I wasn't the best soldier back in those days."

"No thanks necessary, Greg. We all learned a lot during those days. I'm proud of you."

Dempsey shook his hand, and he walked away.

As for Sister Mary Cecilia, she became a favorite at the camp. When they weren't on border duty, some of the soldiers would even travel with their wives to visit her from time to time. Dempsey stayed in touch with her for over twenty years until she passed away. He never forgot what she had done for each and every one of the soldiers with whom she prayed: leave them with fond memories of peace, of being heard, and of being valued.

• • •

Providing team members with a sense of belonging is an admirable goal, but as a leader, you may find yourself asking how exactly you can accomplish that. Following the principle "Give them memories" is a tangible, practical way to create a sense of belonging within your organization.

"Give them memories" is the ongoing practice of providing your subordinates with meaningful experiences from which they will learn and that they will carry with them into the future. The effective leader will set the stage for his or her subordinates to build memories around a breadth of experiences, both positive and negative. The kinds of experiences a leader should provide include:

Successes: Every team member should have memories of what success looks like. How the team accomplished its goal. How the individual himself contributed to that goal. How accomplishing the goal served the higher purpose of the organization. What it felt like to be successful as an individual. What it felt like to be successful as a team. And what it felt like to contribute to the success of the organization.

Failures: Everyone should also have memories of what failure looks like. What the team did wrong, or what it could have done better to achieve the goal. How the individual himself could have acted differently to change the outcome. What effect the failure had on the overall goals of the organization. And the feelings one must manage in the face of failure.

Being cared for: At the core of belonging are a sense of purpose and a sense of safety. When we show our followers that we care about them as individuals and as contributors to our teams, we reinforce the strength of their sense of belonging to the organization.

What right looks like: Doing the right thing isn't always easy. Leaders need to provide their team members with opportunities to learn how to decide what is the right thing to do and carry out those actions, even when doing so is the more difficult route. Your subordinates will walk away with a memory that teaches them a valuable lesson and helps guide their individual moral compasses.

What wrong looks like: Mistakes are bound to happen, and these are often the best learning opportunities. An effective leader presents his or her team with situations where it will be easy to do the wrong thing. Coping with the stress and other feelings associated with realizing the wrong thing was done will not only teach your followers valuable moral lessons, but will provide them with the experience and tools to cope with future losses and failures.

By following the principle "give them memories," a leader takes the first step in building the genuine sense of belonging that is imperative to the success of the organization. These memories motivate your subordinates to contribute to the vision and efforts of the team.

Memories help to inspire and nurture in each individual a genuine commitment to follow the leader in his or her mission to serve the purpose of the organization. To "give them memories" is provide your people with the experiences, lessons, and tools they need in order to make a positive impact on the group and its operations.

CHAPTER 7: **CONNECT EFFORT WITH MEANING**

Leadership Principle #2: Make It Matter

The movie *Saving Private Ryan* takes place during the initial days of the Normandy invasion in June 1944. It is a tale of unimaginable courage and leadership under the harshest of conditions.

A schoolteacher before being drafted, Captain John Miller and nine of his men survive the horrors of the landing on Omaha Beach and are sent to find Private Ryan, a soldier who has landed behind enemy lines with the 101st Air Assault Division and the sole surviving son of a mother who has just lost her other three sons in combat within days of each other. Captain Miller's men are perplexed, and a few are angry that they must risk their lives for this anonymous soldier, but under his leadership they successfully find Private Ryan and bring him to safety—at great cost.

There is a powerful scene at the end of *Saving Private Ryan* in which Captain John Miller, dying of his wounds and having lost eight of his nine men on the mission to find Private Ryan, whispers to Private Ryan, "Earn this!" Captain Miller is telling Private Ryan to make their sacrifices matter.

We all want to believe that what we do matters. That's true whether we're reflecting on our personal life or on our life in the workplace.

One of a leader's responsibilities is to make sense of things for their followers. As "sense makers," leaders help those around them understand how their contributions fit into the organization's accomplishments. They help them appreciate how they matter. The best leaders do this deliberately and the very best do it often.

It's worth noting that the responsibility to "make it matter" is shared by leader and follower. Each of us should recognize that our life can and should matter. Each of us should embrace the fact that we can make a difference—sometimes in big ways, more often in small ways, so that the aggregate of our lives ultimately matters.

However, like most things in leadership, making it matter is an unequal responsibility. Most of the responsibility is on the leader: to explain, to encourage, and to inspire.

If you are a leader, make it matter. For yourself, for those who follow you, and for your team.

• • •

General Dempsey had 32,000 soldiers with him in Baghdad in 2003 and 2004. Their job was to provide a safe environment in which Iraq's political leaders could restore confidence in their government and reestablish basic services like sewage, water, electricity, and trash collection. As that proved more and more difficult, an insurgency emerged, and Dempsey and his soldiers were among its targets.

They began to take casualties in August of 2003, and as they did, they tried to remember their losses in two ways. It was their practice to begin each day with a morning briefing, and at the start of it they would display the fallen soldiers' names on the large screen at the front of the briefing room and pause for a moment of silence. As soon as possible thereafter, they would hold a memorial service with the soldiers' teammates at their forward operating base. Operating bases were spread across Baghdad.

Very soon General Dempsey became dissatisfied and unsettled at these morning briefings with the thought that a lost soldier was remembered one minute and forgotten the next. He wanted something more enduring, something to hold on to. So he tasked his personnel officer to produce two-by-four-inch laminated cards. Each card was carefully prepared to show the photograph and identifying information of the lost soldier. With these cards, Dempsey reasoned, he could carry them with him always.

As time pressed on and casualties mounted, it wasn't long before General Dempsey was unable to carry all the cards with him at once. He decided he needed a place to keep them safe and found a mahogany cigar box for that purpose. Dempsey placed the precious cards, each bearing the memory of a soldier, carefully inside the box. Each day, he would select at random a few cards to carry with him so he could continue to honor those who had fallen under his command. He still does so.

Eventually the box contained a total of 132 cards, and the box itself grew to carry great importance in Dempsey's life. He decided that he wanted to engrave something on the box, but what?

Most of us have seen images of military memorial services. A small wooden box, an inverted rifle topped with a helmet, a pair of boots, and the fallen soldier's dog tags. In the front row of the service sit the soldier's teammates.

A chaplain provides a spiritual reading. The soldier's immediate supervisor, usually a lieutenant or captain, provides some memory of the soldier. And one or two of his peers, his surviving teammates, present a eulogy. And then "Taps" is played.

For General Dempsey, these were heart-wrenching experiences.

Following each ceremony, those in attendance would pass down the row of the soldier's teammates to render their condolences and provide any encouragement they could muster. In the eyes of the fallen soldier's teammates both fear and guilt were visible: fear that they had to go back out into the environment that had taken their teammate and guilt that while their teammate had not survived, somehow they had.

In those early days, and for the first couple of these ceremonies, General Dempsey simply couldn't find the right words to help either himself or his young warriors. And then one early morning, in that contemplative, almost-spiritual period between sleep and wakefulness, he found three simple words. The right words. The words that would later be engraved on his precious mahogany box.

From that morning on, at the conclusion of each memorial service, when he would walk the line of the soldier's teammates, Dempsey would shake the hands of the survivors of the fallen and tell them simply, "Make it matter." And each and every one of them knew exactly what the general meant.

The box, with the phrase engraved across its lid, has been carefully and reverently placed on General Dempsey's desk as the commander of CENTCOM, as the commander of TRADOC, as the chief of staff of the Army, and as the Chairman of the Joint Chiefs of Staff. He has since reflected that "Make it matter" is a phrase that can and should hold meaning in all of our lives, regardless of occupation or status.

• • •

Nobody wants to go to work each day and "punch the clock." At the core of every individual is the desire to feel that the things they do make a difference to the cause they believe in. And when people feel that the things they do make that difference, each individual contributor to the cause, mission, or vision acts decisively and confidently with his best foot forward. To "make it matter" is to provide meaning in the work that our team members are responsible for handling every day.

The three most practical ways for leaders to pass on the belief that what one does for the organization matters begin with themselves, then focus on the team members, and end with the team itself. The ways leaders can "make it matter" include:

1. **Define and allow others to understand who you are.** Leaders at every level must understand who they are individually and within the larger vision of the organization. In describing this, Mike Krzyzewski, head coach of Duke University's men's basketball team, notes that he doesn't want his talented athletes to "leave their egos at the door of the gymnasium." He wants them to bring their egos in and learn to use them not just for themselves but for the team. Coach K is right. As leaders we should blend egos, not eliminate them. The knowledge of where you fit in the organization gives you strength, aligns your values, and encourages you to lead. The drive, passion, and energy you feel should be worn on your sleeve each day to model desirable behavior and as evidence of how one's individual purpose can coexist with the overall vision of the organization.

2. **Make each individual feel that they have the potential to be a better person.** By allowing your subordinates room to grow and fostering collaboration among team members, you encourage the entire team to use their work as a vehicle to the benefit of themselves and the organization. Moreover, if you can be a leader whom others want to emulate, your subordinates will understand what it means to be better people. General Dempsey was fond of telling his colonels, "If

your subordinates don't want to grow up to be you someday, you're not doing your job."

3. **Make sense of things for the team.** It is the leader's responsibility to instruct, to coach, to hold accountable, and, importantly, to "make sense" of what's going on around the team as it seeks to accomplish its goals. Only when the leader shares knowledge can individuals within the organization understand where they fit.

• • •

When General Dempsey took command of the 5,200 soldiers of the Third Armored Cavalry Regiment in 1996 at Fort Carson, Colorado, he found a unit unsettled by transition. They had recently relocated from Fort Bliss, Texas. Much of the leadership had changed during the transition. They had absorbed soldiers from inactivating units at Fort Carson. They were in an unfamiliar place and unfamiliar with the new leadership of the post.

Compounding the issues brought about by the transition was the fact that it came at a time when the Department of the Army had become notorious for publishing numerous detailed, expansive, and mandatory instructions of things that had to be accomplished as a priority by unit commanders and soldiers across the Army. This was not the first time General Dempsey had seen this; in peacetime, everyone develops an opinion about when the armed forces will next be needed, and to do what. Such was the case in 1996. Each headquarters at every level sought to reduce the risk of being wrong about the requirements of the next deployment by adding to the tasks required of subordinate headquarters. But of course, as Dempsey knew, when everything is a priority, nothing is a priority.

At the direction of its higher headquarters, the regiment had developed a "Mission Essential Task List" that included a dozen missions for which the regiment needed to be prepared—everything from "Deliberate Defense" to "Deliberate Attack," from "Hasty Defense" to "Hasty Attack," and from "Movement to Contact" to the traditional cavalry missions of "Screen, Cover, Route and Area Reconnaissance." In reality, there was not enough time nor enough training resources to be able to achieve proficiency in all of these missions. This left junior leaders very frustrated with senior leaders, who they felt were oblivious to the reality of reconciling competing priorities on a day-to-day basis.

So when General Dempsey took command, the first question he was asked by the unit's leaders was how he would prioritize their activities. It was a fair question. But rather than answer it for them, and rather than take the list and simply place the tasks in some descending order of importance, Dempsey gathered his team leaders and asked them, "What's the one thing?" But they weren't exactly sure what he meant. "You know," he quipped, "like in the movie *City Slickers*. What's the one thing that will define your time as a leader in this regiment?"

Dempsey explained that organizations that have identified the one thing most important to them, the one thing they want to do better than everyone else, know how to prioritize and on which elements of their business to focus. A few years later, as Chairman of the Joint Chiefs of Staff, General Dempsey would be asked by the president of the United States how the U.S. military could help address the emerging Ebola crisis in West Africa. Knowing the military's "one thing" as he answered the president's question led to the successful accomplishment of a very high-stakes and rapidly evolving mission. But more on that later.

"So, what's our 'one thing'?" Dempsey again asked his team at Fort Carson. With the input of every team member, they collectively determined what makes a cavalry regiment a cavalry regiment. Essentially, it is the ability to fight for, accumulate, and provide information to the corps commander—the three-star leader of approximately 45,000 soldiers. The cavalry regiment is the corps commander's eyes and ears, and the corps commander makes decisions about the disposition of his forces and whether to attack or defend based in significant measure on the information he receives from his cavalry regiment.

With that as their touchstone, General Dempsey and his team developed the slogan "We are all scouts." Within a regiment of 5,200 men and women are soldiers of myriad skills including scouts, tankers, artillerymen, chemical specialists, logistics specialists, aviators, cooks, and administrative specialists. But for purposes of establishing their "one thing," each of the 5,200 needed to understand that all of them were scouts. Whether on the front lines or in the rear, and whether cooks or mechanics, from that point forward, they knew what was considered important to their regiment's understanding of the environment. They were scouts.

With that settled, General Dempsey assembled a smaller group of key leaders to confront the lengthy Mission Essential Task List. "Of all the missions on this list," he asked, "which most contributes to our ability to provide the corps commander with information?" The answer was the Movement to Contact.

Military missions are determined by how much is known of the enemy about to be confronted. If a great deal is known about the enemy—location, size, armament—then a Deliberate Attack is the appropriate course of action. If less is known about the enemy and more information is required, then a Movement to Contact is appropriate. In this maneuver, the regiment moves forward with the smallest possible force, and as that forward vanguard makes contact with the enemy, the regiment reacts and adapts. With the proper training, and with the confidence that comes from understanding the commander's intent, the regiment adapts faster than the enemy. Interestingly, all Movements to Contact culminate in a transition to either a Hasty Attack or a Hasty Defense. By focusing on mastering the Movement to Contact, leaders necessarily gain a deep appreciation of those missions as well.

For the two years he was in command, General Dempsey led the regiment in seeking to master the Movement to Contact. Anything else they were asked to do they approached as an adaptation from their mastered task: a derivative of the "one thing" they knew unlocked their potential as soldiers and leaders. And by defining the purpose of the team, General Dempsey found a way to "make it matter" for every member of the regiment.

The second principle of leadership, "Make it matter," works in conjunction with the first principle, "Give them memories," to build a culture for healthy, productive, efficient, and effective actions as individuals contributing to the purposes of the team and the vision of the organization. Only those companies, groups, or teams that embrace these principles can expect to build an ethos that will lead their members to productively navigate through their tasks, respond effectively and efficiently to both high- and low-priority missions, and react effectively in crisis situations. As leaders, it is our responsibility to create and maintain this environment.

CHAPTER 8: **THINK ABOUT WHAT YOU'RE NOT THINKING ABOUT**

Leadership Principle #3: Learn to Imagine

In team sports, what most often sets elite athletes apart is the ability to use their imagination in creating opportunities for themselves and for their teammates.

Legendary hockey player Wayne Gretzky once attributed his great success to "skating to where the puck is going, not to where it has been."

University of Connecticut and Olympic women's basketball coach Geno Auriemma says that he looks for "good passers before good shooters" when he's recruiting players, because good passers see things that good shooters often miss.

Imagining has something to do with anticipation and something to do with vision, but that's just part of it.

Imagination is a learned attribute. It's some combination of training, experience, and eventually instinct that produces creativity in complex environments at the speed of teamwork.

Not everyone will agree that "imagining" can be learned. Failures of imagination are common. In fact, after major crises, and even after many "catastrophic successes," leaders will often say, "We never imagined that could happen."

But leaders can learn to imagine if they place the emphasis on "learn."

If they learn to listen and to seek to know what the most junior member of their team knows.

If they learn to be alert for weak signals and to avoid becoming complacent, satisfied with information affirming their beliefs.

If they learn to find advisers who will challenge them, encourage them, surprise them.

If they learn to connect disparate thoughts and to become uncommonly articulate.

If they learn to challenge assumptions and to ask the right questions.

If they learn to become comfortable with complexity and wary of simplicity.

If you're a leader, you will need to exercise your imagination on behalf of your team. But learn first, and then you'll be able to imagine.

Just like an elite athlete.

• • •

When our organizations are presented with the issues that we are most prepared to solve, those duties for which we have long trained and prepared, for which we have documented processes and rule books and methodologies, our experience guides us toward resolution. We rely on carefully developed sets of tried and true procedures as we move forward in handling the issue.

Conversely, when our organizations are faced with challenges for which we have no training or preparation, we may feel paralyzed by our lack of existing processes. It may be difficult to know even where to begin to bring the problem to its solution.

Further, there are times when we feel *somewhat* prepared to handle an issue but are aware that gaps in our abilities and procedures could have a great and negative effect on the outcome. We can have all the preparation in the world, but regardless of the robustness of existing processes, the high level of confidence we may have in our team's capabilities, or the assuredness we may have that a process that led to success in the past will continue to prove successful in the future—and especially if none of these are present—leaders in the new environment should begin by utilizing our third leadership principle: "Learn to imagine."

As reiterated throughout this book, we as leaders must accept and understand that the environment in which we find ourselves leading today is constantly and rapidly changing, and the information we receive is affected by the digital echo. And this has a number of implications on how we run our organizations.

It means that what worked for us before may not work for us now, that the procedures manual on which we relied in the past cannot possibly cover all the issues we will face in the new environment.

It also means that our roles as leaders are continually increasing in complexity as the challenges we face become vaster and more diverse. Some of our roles are changing at their core with the appearance of new technologies. And lastly it means that instead of executing tasks as experts in our fields, we will be asked to solve problems that we may feel only somewhat able to handle. We will be responsible for carrying out tasks and completing missions for which we have no experience whatsoever, and with a lot at stake.

It doesn't mean, however, that our existing processes are no longer relevant. The procedures manual is still valid and still houses useful information by which our organizations operate on a daily basis. Regarding our roles themselves, it's not that they're becoming too great, that we cannot learn new technologies impacting our industries, or that we cannot find and execute real solutions to the different challenges with which we are presented. And it definitely doesn't mean we need to go gain more experience by enrolling in yet another graduate program or taking a lesser position in order to learn how to navigate these tasks.

The solution is that when faced with any task, whether routine or extreme crisis, we must first imagine the possibilities, or "learn to imagine," in order to determine exactly what our team's goal should be in order to solve the problem.

• • •

Well before Ebola became a national issue, General Dempsey listened to the advice of his staff surgeon, Major General Nadja West, to begin learning about the disease. An expert in her field, she predicted with considerable accuracy that the Ebola virus would have massive implications, and though few others in Washington were discussing the disease at the time, she urged General Dempsey to pay attention to it. West recommended he not only learn more about the disease but also convene a team of experts to discuss how the U.S. military might contribute to a broader government campaign to help control it.

The military was very busy at the time. General Dempsey recalls feeling torn between following West's advice and sticking with some of the more immediate and pressing matters on his plate. He knew this wasn't something in which the military would necessarily become involved. He knew he could deflect suggestions that it should become involved. After all, it was not an inherently military mission. General Dempsey knew, however, that the U.S. military possesses unique organizational, logistical, and training capabilities that would be urgently needed should a crisis erupt.

So Dempsey, along with the Joint Chiefs of Staff, decided to put together a planning team to determine what part of the task would be most appropriate for the military. They would need to know what resources were readily available and how long it would take to prepare them to deploy, and they would need to identify the opportunity costs to their other commitments around the world. As anyone in business or the military is aware, our organizational ecosystem is affected when we must pull resources to handle a crisis situation. In addition to the research on preparation and costs, Dempsey gathered experts on infectious disease from academia and from the Centers for Disease Control and Prevention, as well as Intelligence and State Department experts on West Africa. He also brought the military commander in Africa into the discussions so that he would learn along with the team.

As General Dempsey's staff surgeon had predicted, the Ebola epidemic ultimately escalated to the point of crisis and threatened to spill over into the homeland. The president convened his National Security Council to assess the situation and determine if there were options for government agencies to contribute to its resolution.

The military was ready. General Dempsey and his team had already gained the knowledge they needed. They had established relationships with those who would carry the biggest share of the task. They had consulted with two of our European allies who had similar interests in West Africa. They knew what they could contribute, how quickly, and at what cost to their missions elsewhere. Because they had imagined a future where their "one thing" would be required, they knew how to apply their resources—and especially their knowledge—to this particular situation.

Dempsey and his team presented their well-developed case to the president.

"I suggested that military medical personnel were trained for myriad medical challenges including infectious disease," General Dempsey recalls, "but that pulling significant numbers of medics from within the armed forces would create a readiness problem."

The president agreed with the concern and asked if the team had come up with any other options. Of course, they had.

Rather than using its own medical staff, General Dempsey offered that the military could provide what was most lacking in the crisis, and what the American armed forces do better than anyone else in the world: set up an operations center manned and equipped to process and share information, establish a transportation hub to monitor and coordinate the flow of logistics, and establish a training base for the hundreds of international medical volunteers eager to assist in the crisis. In other words, the one thing the military was best positioned to bring to the fight against Ebola was a forum for coordination.

The president agreed.

To jump-start the effort, the Army deployed the two-star commander of U.S. Army Africa from Vicenza, Italy. Later he would be replaced by a two-star commander of division headquarters from Fort Campbell, Kentucky. The Army envisioned an effort of approximately 2,500 soldiers. Their marching orders were to facilitate coordination of the effort to fight Ebola, to provide an operations center, and to establish open and transparent relationships with U.S. and international relief organizations. They would assist in the management of logistics, construct a training facility, and provide training to medical personnel in how to operate safely within the Ebola hot zone. They established a single limiting principle as their way of articulating risk: no U.S. military personnel would enter the Ebola hot zone, defined as the interiors of facilities actively treating individuals with the virus.

With that guidance, the two commanders deployed to Liberia and accomplished their mission. The military provided those things it can bring faster and better to crises than anyone in the world—coordination, logistics, and training—and empowered those in the task force to adapt within the intent and limiting principle articulated.

They accomplished the Ebola mission without degrading their readiness elsewhere.

• • •

The third leadership principle, "Learn to imagine," refers to creative problem solving and the ways in which leaders should work to reimagine how their teams' abilities can be strategically utilized in a variety of conditions.

As leaders we must avoid assuming that the first answer is the best answer. We cannot blindly follow existing procedures simply because they have worked in the past. Our environment is changing too quickly and our challenges are becoming too complex. We must reach beyond our regular lines of thinking and acting, rethink the ways in which we can apply our teams' abilities, and empower our people to help us define the paths to success.

CHAPTER 9: **PREVENT DECISION PARALYSIS**

Leadership Principle #4: Develop a Bias for Action

In one of many clever moments in *Through the Looking-Glass*, Lewis Carroll depicts Alice running hard but remaining in the same spot. Alice is both exhausted and exasperated. The Red Queen, lounging under a nearby tree, is amused.

> Alice looked round her in great surprise. "Why, I do believe we've been under this tree the whole time! Everything's just as it was!"
>
> "Of course it is," said the Queen, "what would you have it?"
>
> "Well, in *our* country," said Alice, still panting a little, "you'd generally get to somewhere else—if you ran very fast for a long time, as we've been doing."
>
> "A slow sort of country!" said the Queen. "Now, *here*, you see, it takes all the running *you* can do, to keep in the same place. If you want to get somewhere else, you must run at least twice as fast as that!"[17]

---

17. Lewis Carroll, Alice's Adventures in Wonderland & Through the Looking-Glass
(1871; New York: Bantam Classics, reissue ed. 2006), pp. 134–5.

The year was 1871, and in this scene Carroll was alluding to an evolutionary theory of the time, which posited that organisms must constantly adapt and evolve to survive while pitted against ever-evolving opposing organisms in an ever-changing environment.

Sound familiar? If the Red Queen was right about how fast we needed to adapt in the nineteenth century, what would she say today?

As a leader in today's environment, you may not find yourself responsible for the outcome of an ongoing evolutionary contest, but you will find yourself responsible for the outcome of a contest for the success, the trust, and the confidence of those who follow you in an ever-evolving, ever-changing environment.

And to prevail in that contest, you need to develop a bias for action.

A bias for action is a leadership instinct based on the belief that in order to decide, you must learn, and in order to learn, you must alter the status quo.

A bias for action is a leadership instinct that mitigates decision paralysis and helps you avoid the endless pursuit of that one exquisite piece of information that seems to be all that stands between you and clarity.

A bias for action is the recognition that, in our complex world, learning is active and iterative. We act, we assess, and we act again.

A bias for action is the recognition that facts are vulnerable and that speed matters in the era of digital echoes.

A bias for action won't solve all of your leadership challenges, but it will energize your organization, keep you alert to both vulnerabilities and opportunities, and illuminate the often-hidden cost of inaction.

The military has a saying: "Lead, follow, or get out of the way." That's a bias for action.

• • •

In a well-known anecdote about Albert Einstein, he is quoted as saying that if he had sixty minutes to save the world, he would spend fifty-five of those minutes understanding the problem and five minutes fixing it. Many past leadership theories have echoed Einstein, encouraging leaders to carefully analyze problems before taking action. Contemporary leadership theories, however, must understand the changing nature of time and how it affects us as leaders and the decisions we make in our organizations.

Faced with a sea of data, ever-multiplying technologies, and the digital echo, we have a tendency to halt all motion so that we may back away from situations and try to understand all their moving parts. We develop insatiable appetites for information and sometimes absurd desires for more (read: better) options to present themselves so we can be certain of our decisions. We mobilize our teams to cultivate more and more information, hoping that the perfect solution exists among the clutter.

But how much time are we willing to spend on research (without action), and will the research still be valid by the time we are ready to make a decision? What do we do with all of that information once we have it? How do we sort through it? And how can we tell a bad solution from a good one, or a great solution from a crazy idea?

As a leader facing an issue or crisis, we may have a sense that a dichotomy exists wherein we must either (a) sit back and analyze the issue and its potential solutions or (b) seize control of the issue immediately by taking possibly misguided action. We always want to be sure we are making the best, most informed decisions possible, and we do all we can to avoid acting in ways that will be detrimental to our team or the organization. Nine times out of ten, an intelligent leader will analyze a situation before taking a broad, sweeping action that may be catastrophic to his team or organization. Why push forward when you may hardly understand what the most desirable outcome might be, let alone what steps the team needs to take to get there?

But leaders cannot allow themselves to become paralyzed by a search for the perfect answer while information flows and technology updates at ever-increasing speeds. Leaders are now facing scenarios that require action in the moment, before significant changes can occur in the environment and before we can possibly fully analyze the problem. The longer we take to respond to catalysts, the more our environment adapts, and the less we understand about the issue and how to solve it. So we must act quickly but intelligently.

• • •

In March 2004, the 32,000 soldiers of General Dempsey's First Armored Division prepared to transfer responsibility for security in Baghdad to the soldiers of the First Cavalry Division. General Dempsey and his troops had been in Baghdad for a year, and it was time to go home. Home, for most of them, was one of several bases in Germany.

An advance party of several thousand soldiers had already been sent back to Germany to ensure that barracks and motor pools were ready for the arrival of the larger group of soldiers. Family members were planning welcome-home ceremonies, and some were making travel arrangements for the vacations they would take when their soldiers came back from Iraq. Others had received orders for follow-on assignments in the United States, and they would begin out-processing following block leave.

A ceremony marking the completion of the transfer of responsibility from General Dempsey and his 32,000 soldiers to the First Cavalry Division was scheduled for April 7 at the large "crossed sabres" parade field in Baghdad. But in preparation for the switch, hands had been changed across Baghdad neighborhoods up to two weeks prior.

Commanders of one-thousand-soldier battalions and three-thousand-soldier brigades from the two divisions worked together to complete a checklist of activities necessary to certify each transfer. Relationships with Iraqi Security Force partners, local governing officials, tribal leaders, and religious leaders were carefully passed. Specialized equipment was transferred. As battalions completed their transfers, they began the long convoy to Kuwait, where their remaining equipment would be sent back to Germany on ships. Hundreds of soldiers were moved to Balad Air Base north of Baghdad, where they would fly home on Air Force aircraft.

In the midst of the changeover, General Dempsey's division was spread among Baghdad, Kuwait, Balad, and Germany. And on April 4, less than seventy-two hours prior to the completion of the transfer of responsibility, it all fell apart.

Shia militia in Baghdad and Iraq, along with Sunni insurgents in Al Anbar Province, staged an uprising against their provisional government and against the U.S. troops stationed there. General Dempsey's division learned that the highway they had been using to supply their forces from Kuwait had been severed by Shia militia. In the eastern part of Baghdad, Sadr City was in flames. West of Baghdad, Fallujah was under Sunni insurgent control. They soon realized that Baghdad was isolated from the rest of the country.

With Iraqi sovereignty expected to be restored to a newly elected government that coming June, it wasn't only the division's timetable that was put at risk by the uprising. The entire mission in Iraq was at risk.

In the early morning of April 4, General Dempsey walked out of the back of his headquarters, located in the center of

Baghdad International Airport. To the north he could see the dark black smoke of twelve evenly spaced oil fires, a sure sign that a U.S. convoy of five-thousand-gallon fuel trucks had been ambushed. From the east he could hear the unmistakable sound of a firefight. He knew that to the west the Marines were embroiled in a tough fight with Sunni insurgents. And that earlier that morning, two bridges across the supply line to Kuwait had been demolished, effectively blocking the highway.

General Dempsey was also well aware that the coalition had no forces in reserve. All of the forces in Iraq were committed to other geographic responsibilities or to other tasks. Except for his forces.

The soldiers and leaders designated to replace them in Baghdad had arrived. Dempsey still had more than 10,000 soldiers of First Armored Division in Baghdad in various stages of transition and another 2,000 or so in Kuwait. He knew that in an emergency he could recall the soldiers already home in Germany, and he had 2,500 exceptional scouts of the Second Light Cavalry Regiment from Fort Polk, Louisiana, still attached to his division.

Anticipating what he knew would soon be asked of him—to remain with his troops in Iraq for several more months to quell the uprising—Dempsey first had to stop any further movement south to Kuwait and by air from Balad.

Fortunately his two deputies, Brigadier General Mark Hertling and Brigadier General Mike Scaparrotti, were at his headquarters that morning for a review of the division's progress toward redeployment. The three huddled.

"We've got a few challenges in sorting all of this out," Dempsey told them. "We *know* it's becoming increasingly likely we're going to be told to stay in Iraq longer, but no one is going to tell us that until it's approved all the way to the White House. We also know that if we stop our redeployment convoys and flights, it will signal to both our soldiers and their families that something is wrong. But if we don't stop these movements, we may not be able to regroup quickly enough to get back into the fight in time to make a difference."

Complicating matters even further was that in the early months of the war one of the division's sister units had been extended, and it had caused a significant—and embarrassing—morale problem that had received a great deal of media coverage. Neither the Army nor the Department of Defense wanted a repeat of that incident.

Furthermore, making a decision to keep soldiers in Iraq beyond twelve months was a big step for an administration that was counting on the mission ending, not extending.

The trio knew that the politics inside and outside Iraq were hypersensitive at the moment and that they would be expected to await instructions before doing anything to change their mission. They also knew that every passing hour allowed the militia to become further entrenched in the key cities of southern Iraq and the population to become intimidated. The complexity and speed of the evolving crisis argued for them to act.

So they acted.

They decided to stop the movement of soldiers to Kuwait and to suspend flights from Balad based on the increased risk caused by the uprising. General Dempsey informed Lieutenant General Rick Sanchez, commander of coalition forces in Iraq, that he was suspending the movement of his forces and would reevaluate the decision daily.

Dempsey explained that he knew the difficulty Sanchez faced in determining how to deal with the uprising and let him know that Dempsey, along with the other leaders of the First Armored Division, were assessing what it would take to regroup to provide Sanchez with options. Dempsey asked Sanchez for a quick decision on whether the division would remain in Iraq so that he could communicate with his soldiers and their families. For many reasons, he didn't expect a quick decision.

Fortunately, General Dempsey was previously scheduled to meet with the CENTCOM commander, General John Abizaid, the next day. He would be attuned to options that might exist outside Iraq and, importantly, to issues in Washington that might impact any decision. So Dempsey called Abizaid's executive officer to give him his assessment and to give Abizaid notice that he would be seeking guidance the next day.

After another late-night discussion with his brigadiers, Dempsey scheduled a meeting of all battalion commanders, brigade commanders, and their command sergeants major for the next day following his meeting with General Abizaid.

Meanwhile, the situation in Baghdad had become worse. The Marines needed reinforcements for the fight in Fallujah, and the only other Marines in Iraq were tied down south of Baghdad in what later became known as the "triangle of death." General Jim Mattis called General Dempsey to ask if the First Armored Division could extend south of Baghdad so that he could take those Marines to join the fight in Fallujah. Dempsey told Mattis that he could and would make this recommendation to both Lieutenant General Sanchez and General Abizaid the next day.

Further south, in Karbala, Wasit, Diwaniyah, and Najaf provinces, the Shia militia had taken over provincial government buildings and were threatening the United States' Polish coalition partners. Due to Polish government caveats, the Poles—who are good fighters—were limited in what they could do. Specifically, they could conduct defensive but not offensive operations. If offensive operations were to be conducted to restore control of these three provinces to Iraqi government control, it would have to be U.S. forces conducting them.

When General Dempsey met with General Abizaid, they compared assessments of the situation. "It's bad," Abizaid began.

"The provisional government of Iraq is fragile, and at home this will be a serious setback. I know you're already aware that we may need you and your soldiers to stay here until we stabilize the situation, and I know how tough that will be on your soldiers and their families. I need to know if you can do it."

General Dempsey appreciated the question from a leader who was always attuned to the human dimension of warfare. "We can, sir," Dempsey responded. "But to do it, and to keep faith with my soldiers, I need three things. First, I need to keep the unit together. Don't parcel out my battalions and brigades to thicken things elsewhere. If you keep us together, we'll respond together. Second, I need you to give us a mission. Don't just keep us sitting in Baghdad. Give us something to do. And third, most importantly, let me entrust my soldiers and their families with information. If they hear about this on CNN before they hear it from me, we'll be in trouble."

"Do you have a mission in mind?" Abizaid asked. "I do, sir," Dempsey replied. "Release the Marines in South Baghdad to Jim Mattis and give that sector to me. Besides the South Baghdad mission, task me to restore control of Karbala, Wasit, Diwaniyah, and Najaf provinces. Give me authority to coordinate with the Polish forces to our south and assist them in dealing with the Shia militia and keeping our line of communication to Kuwait open."

"How long will you need?" he asked. "We can get it done in ninety days," Dempsey said. General Abizaid nodded. "Okay, Marty. I can give you two of those three right now. We'll keep your unit intact, and we'll give you the missions you suggest. As far as getting ahead of the Pentagon with letting your soldiers and their families know what's happening, just use your judgment. God bless you and your troops."

En route from that meeting to the one with battalion commanders, brigade commanders, and their command sergeants major, General Dempsey called his two brigadiers from his vehicle.

"Okay, men," he said. "Turn the division around."

The rest of the ride, General Dempsey prepared himself for the next meeting. He knew that bringing back soldiers who had already redeployed home would be extraordinarily hard on them and on their families. His next call would be to his wife, Deanie, to share all of this with her. She would have a huge role to play in making sure that the families were on board and would be cared for during the extension. Dempsey knew that the families back home would already have an instinct that something wasn't right. In these times of ubiquitous communications, Dempsey knew that in a way, we bring our families to war with us.

The meeting with his battalion commanders, brigade commanders, and command sergeants major was one of the most memorable experiences of Dempsey's long career. It was a group of about seventy-five senior leaders. Everyone knew what was coming, and the tension in the room was palpable.

General Dempsey spoke without slides, images, or maps. This was to be a conversation with his family of the past year. He began by describing the situation as they understood it. He explained that the entire mission was at risk. He reassured them that their division had accomplished its part of the task, pausing to reflect on the fact that they had lost almost one hundred soldiers during their time in Baghdad. Dempsey explained that they were about to be asked to do something both very difficult and truly extraordinary.

"We are going to be asked to turn the division around, to bring more than a thousand soldiers back from Germany, to reconstitute a force that was almost out of Iraq and get it back in the fight to restore control of southern Iraq to the government of Iraq." Dempsey acknowledged that this would put enormous pressure on them as leaders but expressed his certainty that if they approached this challenge as they had every other challenge over the past twelve months, then this event would become a glorious part of their unit's history.

General Dempsey told them that it wouldn't be right to have sacrificed so much over the past year to expel one tyrant just to see him replaced by another form of tyranny. He acknowledged that their families would take this news hard. He told them that he intended to send Brigadier General Mark Hertling back to Germany the next day to meet over the course of the next week with the families on each kaserne. He told them that the USA-REUR commander, General B. B. Bell, had promised to break down the barriers to help the families recover deposits, alter plans, and adjust airline reservations. He told them that they would decide—they and their families—whether this would be a positive or a negative moment in the division's history. He informed them that none of this could be made public until the Pentagon announced it, but that he wanted them—and their families—to hear it from him and not from the news media. General Dempsey finished by asking them to keep the information among themselves, and told them he was proud of them.

There were questions, mostly about the mission. Dempsey explained that they had three tasks, that the tasks were very different, and that he would count on each of them to continue to learn and adapt as they accomplished them.

The Second Light Cavalry Regiment would move to Wasit, Diwaniyah, and Najaf provinces and recapture them from the Shia militia. The Second Brigade would move to southern Baghdad and take over responsibility for that sector from the Marines. The First Brigade would move to Karbala and Babil provinces to conduct offensive operations to restore control with the Polish partners.

General Dempsey told them that there would be an ongoing and parallel political negotiation among U.S. diplomats, Iraqi government officials, and Shia political leaders that, at times, they would need to support. They would have met their objectives when the provisional government of Iraq's appointed officials were restored to authority, when the Shia militia in southern Iraq had disbanded and its leaders were back within the political process, and when the Sunni insurgents in southern Baghdad were no longer capable of contributing to the fight in Fallujah.

General Dempsey noted that over the past year, this group of men and women had developed a remarkable rapport. He told them that he expected them to collaborate with one another in the execution of these new missions, to cross-talk and share resources, and to make decisions within his intent.

"Don't wait for me to approve every movement or adaptation you need to make," Dempsey told them. "Keep me informed, let me know if you need something that only I can provide, and I'll do the same for you. It won't do us any good to accomplish two out of three of these missions. We need to work together to accomplish all three."

The next day, Brigadier General Mark Hertling returned to Germany. There he teamed with Deanie and with General B. B. Bell to empower spouses with the information they needed in order to understand why this extension and the mission were so important. These three were able to build and sustain trust among the division's leaders and their families; the extension didn't generate a single negative media story, despite the fact that these families would have to continue to sacrifice and the division would continue to take casualties.

It wasn't until three days later that the Pentagon announced the extension. By that time, everyone in the division and their families had been notified.

In Iraq, General Dempsey's other deputy, Brigadier General Mike Scaparrotti, was busy reconstituting the division. Equipment that had been wrapped for shipment in Kuwait was unwrapped, convoys were returning to Baghdad, and personnel were reintegrated with their units and were prepared for combat.

General Dempsey would travel from unit to unit across

Baghdad and make his own assessment of their readiness. At one stop, he was busy explaining why this extension was so important when a young staff sergeant interrupted him.

"With all due respect, sir, you don't have to explain all of this to us. We've been through a lot together, and we trust you."

Moved by these words, Dempsey decided the division was ready. The staff sergeant went on, "So, sir, if it's all the same to you, you go on and do what you have to do, and we'll get about the business of doing what we have to do." General Dempsey swelled with pride.

At another stop, another sergeant told Dempsey of a conversation he'd had with his wife on the phone that morning. The sergeant was apologizing to his wife for missing his daughter's high school prom and graduation and his young son's soccer season. His wife scolded him for apologizing and told him that she had been to Brigadier General Hertling's briefing. "You need to concentrate on your mission and getting home safely. We'll take care of business back here," she said. Empowering the families with the information necessary for them to understand the task at hand had been the right thing to do.

Ninety days later, General Dempsey's division had accomplished its new mission, and they once again prepared to head home. They had lost another forty soldiers during the extension. All losses during the deployment were tragic, these last forty especially so.

There are many lessons to be taken from the First Armored Division's actions between April and July 2004. They made it through this period because they worked together to achieve clarity of purpose, unity of effort, shared power, constant communication, and—most of all—trust. They didn't do everything right in Baghdad during this deployment and its extension. But during the dark days of April, when asked to do the inconceivable, they acted. And they mostly got it right.

• • •

Rarely in organizations do we find ourselves at a standstill or in a position in which we simply carry out daily tasks without facing problems or crises. Issues may be low priority, affecting very few people in very minor ways, or they may be full-blown, all-hands-on-deck threats to the organization. In General Dempsey's case, it was sending 32,000 soldiers back into war. In the new environment, leaders must understand that in order to assert and sustain power both in steady times and in the face of great challenge, their organizations need to maintain a proactive mind-set and treat every catalyst with a bias for action.

The immediate actions we take in response to catalysts need not always be dramatic, but some action is almost always required. As leaders, we need to ask ourselves what we can do right now to make an impact in solving the issue, sometimes without fully comprehending where that action may lead. In order to interact with the new environment, though, we need to change and evolve along with it, rather than attempt to fight it. We need to act based on the information we have, not remain immobile waiting for "better" options to emerge. If we adopt a mind-set whereby we act, assess, and then act again, we can steadily work toward conquering the challenges we face.

Actively engaging with issues to influence their outcomes early, before they evolve in ways that may prove even more counter to our interests, is paramount in the new environment. We need a bias for action not only to be decisive in our reactions to catalysts, but also as part of our overall strategy in building and sustaining our power. Without it, companies and countries alike will simply be outpaced.

CHAPTER 10: **COLLABORATE AT EVERY LEVEL OF THE ORGANIZATION**

Leadership Principle #5: Co-create Context

General Dempsey is a Jersey boy, or at least he was. So, as he left beautiful and historic Congress Hall in Cape May on his way back to Washington DC, he wasn't surprised at the volume of traffic he soon encountered. Fortunately, when his chosen route became congested, Waze offered him an alternative. His fellow travelers—several hundred of them—were sharing information on how he might get to his destination faster. They were "co-creating the context" of the decisions he was making about his trip.

Decisions are always made in some context. As a result, they produce second- and sometimes even third-order effects that inevitably affect future decisions. So gaining the best possible understanding of context before making decisions produces better decisions.

For example, military commanders in Iraq and Afghanistan quickly learned that destroying infrastructure used by enemy forces might make perfect sense militarily, but in that environment and in that kind of conflict the adverse effect on local civilians could be detrimental to the long-term objective of gaining their support and ending the campaign. The decision to destroy buildings, bridges, and markets (and even Taliban smuggling routes, as we saw in chapter 3) or leave them intact depended on an appreciation of context.

An understanding of context is best achieved when there is collaboration at every level of the organization. We call this the "co-creation of context" to make the point that it is everyone's responsibility and to highlight—again—that speed matters in the era of digital echoes.

Back to General Dempsey's drive home and the alternate route offered by Waze.

Waze is context built in real time by anonymous participants without ownership in decisions or their outcomes. But what if context could be produced at the speed of Waze by participants who feel like they belong and have a stake in the success of the organization? Decisions would clearly be better. Typically, senior leaders gain an understanding of context by "pulling" it from within their organizations. In the military, senior leaders publish "priority information requirements" (PIR), which tell subordinates what these leaders want to know. But we would be more effective as leaders if individuals within the organization were organized and encouraged to tell us not just what we say we want to know but also what they think we need to know.

Furthermore, when lists of desired information are generated at the top of an organization, they're usually focused on things that could go wrong, things that could take the organization "off plan." Few organizations, especially big ones, ask their junior members about opportunities the organization may be missing. Establishing processes to allow our organizations to co-create context will produce better decisions and, under the right leadership conditions, produce them faster. Better decisions made faster is what we need in an era that requires us to overcome the inertia of complexity and react quickly in the face of change.

• • •

Finding ways to gain the support and insight of the entire organization is imperative. Leaders must recognize that though their experience lends them a valuable discerning eye, a real and complete understanding of complex issues requires perspectives from every part of the organization. We can't expect to solve our problems effectively until we have this thorough grasp of the problem.

In discovering options, the best ideas do not always come from the top of the organization; in fact, it is often the team members on the front line who have the most creative solutions—which may turn out to be the ones that save us.

Our challenge as leaders is to empower the entire organization to take part in understanding the problem the team is facing and to encourage individuals at all levels to suggest potential ways to reach our desired outcomes.

Remember General Dempsey's young captain on the Afghanistan-Pakistan border? After explaining to the general the difference between hierarchical organizations and decentralized networks, he went on to suggest that although the Army had gone to great lengths and spared no effort to push capability "to the edge," it had not done nearly enough to harvest the resulting knowledge produced there.

When General Dempsey asked the young captain what he needed in order to accomplish his mission under the very harsh conditions of the Hindu Kush, he was pleased that the captain didn't present him with a "wish list" of resources. The captain already had an impressive array of weaponry giving him a significant advantage in both day and night operations.

He had access to the highest levels of intelligence and was able to maintain accurate "situational awareness" of who and what was operating on the ground and in the air near his combat outpost. His soldiers were networked with a suite of the most modern communications equipment. His resupply needs were being met. On reflection, General Dempsey realized that this twenty-eight-year-old captain had more tools at his immediate disposal than he himself had had during his time in Baghdad, with 32,000 soldiers spread out over seven hundred square kilometers of urban sprawl.

What the young man did seek, though, was Dempsey's assurances that what the captain knew in his small piece of Afghanistan was making its way back to the various headquarters above him and all the way to the Pentagon, so that the top brass had an understanding of the challenges he faced. Dempsey couldn't give him that assurance.

Although the U.S. military had done a superb job of empowering the lowest tactical levels with every possible capability available, giving its soldiers a decided edge against their enemies, the military had not yet figured out how to harvest the knowledge available at the edge in a timely and effective manner. In an organization spread from the Potomac River to the Himalayas, gaining a common understanding of context remained challenging.

General Dempsey realized that often—perhaps even usually—the most important piece of information that a senior leader needs is one that comes from the edge of the organization, not from its center. And we can be sure we're accomplishing what we set out to accomplish only if we insist upon and enable the co-creation of context throughout the organization.

Easier said than done, but as technology has improved, it has produced opportunities for leaders at all levels to co-create context and in so doing dramatically improve performance.

This leadership principle highlights the leader's responsibility to harvest the knowledge that exists throughout the organization and to build a broader understanding of the ways the team's abilities can be aligned to solve the problem. Rather than the leader bearing the immense responsibility of discovering solutions unilaterally or alone, solving the problem becomes a matter of narrowing down a diverse list of creative solutions proposed by the team. The leader's expertise is applied to decision making and directing, rather than controlling and dictating.

Let's look at an example of the importance of context.

Two decades after McDonald's dropped its case against Ori and the McVegan campaign, things appeared to come full circle. In 2015 McDonald's CEO, Don Thompson, left the conglomerate to join the board of directors at up-and-coming vegan food start-up Impossible Foods. That move would've been completely unthinkable back in the midnineties, but veganism is no longer on the fringe of society. In fact, Impossible Foods has received more than $100 million in Silicon Valley venture capital funding. That's not because the financiers have a soft spot for animal rights or environmentalism, or are do-gooders in general. Following in the footsteps of the radical inclusion philosophy of Vegan Action twenty years ago, Impossible Foods is taking a counterintuitive approach to its business model.

Put yourself for a moment at the head of Impossible Foods. Your mission is to make the best possible veggie burger. You have at your disposal a biochemistry team that can help you get the right texture and taste. How would you go about developing your product and marketing it? What approach would you take? Take a few moments to consider your plan of attack, because it's not as simple as it may first appear.

If you're like most people, you'd start out by doing your homework. You'd survey the competition—conduct taste tests of the best soy and portobello burgers out there—and come up with a product that feels and tastes better. Then you would reach out to the retailers most likely to carry such a product, like Whole Foods and online vegan outlets, and try to get it recognized as the industry standard.

That's the wrong approach, and not the one taken by Impossible Foods. For one thing, the company would never have been able to get substantial VC funding to come up with the best veggie burger; there's nothing new or exciting about that. But more important, reaching out to vegetarians and health-conscious shoppers misses the point. What if you turned the business plan on its head and took a completely different approach, one that takes account of the broader context?

Meet Impossible Foods' founder and CEO, Pat Brown. He's not your typical Silicon Valley entrepreneur. Well into his sixties, tall, with a runner's build, this former Stanford biochemistry professor looks and sounds the part of the stereotypical hippie. He has been a vegetarian since the 1970s and likes to chat about "mature technology photosynthesis" and "carbon stored in biomass." Hearing him speak about the food industry, you'd think he was a Green Party candidate: "There's a tremendous influence of the very institutions that we're trying to disrupt, which have a lot of control in government."

In 2010 Brown tried to get his message across to the public by creating a National Research Council workshop in Washington called "The Role of Animal Agriculture in a Sustainable 21st Century Global Food System." If you haven't heard of it, you're not the only one. Virtually no one cared. Brown knew there had to be a better way.

Instead of criticizing the meat industry, he decided to emulate it. He noted that people who make and sell beef burgers don't preach at their customers; they give them the product they want. Brown understood that in order to make a difference, he would have to be inclusive: he needed to deliver a vegetarian alternative for meat eaters. His core competition, he realized, was not other veggie burgers. He wasn't trying to give vegetarians a better culinary experience (though that was a welcome side effect); they were already sold. Brown was looking to convert meat-and-potatoes guys with no interest in vegetarianism or the environment.

Impossible Foods' goal is to replicate—even improve on—a top-grade beef burger. "All you have to do," Brown explains, "is make a product that the current consumers of meat and dairy prefer to what they're getting now." With modern science there's no reason you can't create a vegetable-based product that convincingly mimics its meat-based alternative.

And instead of introducing the burger at Whole Foods or at vegan restaurants, Brown decided to roll out his creation at restaurants that serve both carnivores and herbivores. And not just any restaurants: the Impossible Burger made its debut at upscale foodie havens whose chefs each put their own unique spin on it. In creating their own mouthwatering versions of the Impossible Burger—with house-made buns and toppings like caramelized onions, truffle cream, Gruyère cheese, mushroom puree, and kochujang aioli (whatever that is)—the chefs were co-creating the context of the Impossible Burger, helping to position it as not an ordinary veggie burger but an alternative for meat-eating gourmands.

CHAPTER 11: **EXPAND THE CIRCLE**

Leadership Principle #6: Relinquish Control to
Build and Sustain Power

The era of digital echoes requires leaders to develop an instinct for inclusion, an uncommon commitment to reach beyond collaboration all the way to trust, a willingness to purposefully relinquish control to preserve power.

Because everyone is listening, everyone is watching, everyone is scrutinizing, all the time, everywhere, at the speed of memes—heightening interest, stirring emotions, raising expectations, and creating both vulnerabilities and opportunities.

It's not science fiction. It's part of our lives. Today. It makes this an exciting time to lead.

In these times, we can choose to see the world as a perpetually competitive arena where interactions result in winner-take-all outcomes, or we can see the world as an increasingly and inevitably collaborative space where common benefits accrue through common costs.

Of course, it's easier to explain the competitive nature of the world than it is to explain the collaborative nature of the world.

It's easier to describe a "clean" win than a shared accomplishment.

But seeking absolute, concrete dominance is a costly strategy, certainly difficult in the past and increasingly unsustainable today. Additionally, concentrated power is making our world more dangerous: as countries concentrate control, their communities and citizens become more divided and insular. Solving problems by emphasizing exclusion, jealously husbanding power, and aspiring to greater control is producing suboptimal, fragile, and costly outcomes.

Rather than attempting to dominate, we suggest that leaders instead learn to relinquish control. Instead of grasping at the control we may feel slipping through our fingers, we should embrace the changing nature of power. We should allow control to flow out of our hands and into the capable, trained hands of the members of our organizations.

The overall goal of leadership is to increase effectiveness and build a history of successes within the organization. In order to champion these successes, a leader must build and preserve power and order within the team. Power affords the leader the ability to act, and order provides predictability in the team's actions. Preserving power and order, over the long term and at a sustainable cost, is the biggest challenge we face as leaders in our changing world.

Without power, we cannot expect to lead. But leaders often exert control when it is not needed, and at a cost that is not justified. In this new environment, concentrations of power cannot endure. While power remains necessary for effective leadership, the path to sustainable power is no longer through control.

Real power is measured not in degree of control but rather in the ability to find optimum, affordable, enduring solutions to complex problems.

In Iraq and Afghanistan, for example, U.S. military leaders and diplomats learned that to preserve their power to influence tribal, religious, and political leaders they had to willingly and transparently relinquish control over time.

Control is seductive because it creates the perception of power.

Control often produces narrow, suboptimal solutions that struggle to endure.

Control is expensive.

We're not arguing that leaders should cede all control. We are arguing that in these times of complexity, speed, and scrutiny, the best solutions, the most affordable solutions, the most enduring solutions will be the product of inclusion.

Carefully developed and persistently nurtured, inclusion creates speed and efficiency in the workplace, in our communities, in our countries, and in the world. As leaders we need to employ inclusion in order to sustain our system of alliances and partnerships. We need to build a consensus with our teams and with like-minded partners toward longer-term solutions at sustainable levels of effort.

Order and inclusion need to exist in tension with each other, supporting each other in an appropriate balance where both are adequately represented. Order and inclusion can and should be complementary. To build and maintain power, we need both control and inclusion.

When a leader feels he is losing his power, the instinct is to hold on more tightly to reclaim that power—to reestablish order through the imposition of control. Traditionally, power was maintained by concentrating and building control, and in the new, rapidly changing environment in which we operate today, powerful governments, companies, and individuals are finding it increasingly easy to amass vast amounts of control. But having too much control can be a liability for leaders, teams, and organizations alike.

The energy sector provides a good example.

To hear the traditional gas and electrical energy professionals talk about it, the energy sector faces three urgent and converging challenges:

1. Dramatic changes in the industry related to techno-
   logical change and national decarbonization goals
2. Replacing an aging workforce
3. A demand for innovative leadership

For most of the last century, the energy sector has enjoyed a relative monopoly. However, that monopoly is rapidly eroding. Nineteen states have adopted competitive energy markets and the other thirty-one are in various stages of reforming their regulatory structures.

Jim Rogers, former CEO and president of America's largest energy company, Duke Energy, describes the changing energy environment as "the democratization of electricity." Customers are increasingly going off the gas and electric grid in favor of renewable energy. As an example, he notes that 1.3 gigawatts of demand came "off the roof" in solar energy last year, and that demand will not return to the traditional utilities. Moreover, he asserts that a 1 percent decline in demand produces a 3 percent increase in cost, shared by customers and producers.

Jim also describes an industry where there have been few positive interactions with customers. "Everyone," he says, "knows the cost of a gallon of gas. No one knows the cost of a kilowatt-hour of electricity." The result is suspicion, mistrust, and an adversarial relationship with customers, who have felt imprisoned by a lack of choice in energy providers.

At the same time, alternative and renewable energy sources have become increasingly affordable and practical.

Together these factors have made the cost of maintaining control of the traditional natural gas and electric utilities prohibitively high. Jim's answer: utilities need to take on the task of designing customer experience with energy.

Stated another way, to preserve their power—their market

share and influence—they must relinquish some control to renewables and to their customers.

Dean Seavers became president of National Grid in 2014. National Grid is among the nation's top five electricity and natural gas utilities, servicing one of its most challenging markets in the Northeast.

In his vision statement for National Grid, titled "The Democratization of Energy," Dean reflects on the tremendous change facing his industry and outlines three imperatives for managing that change: "First, we must put customers in charge. Second, we must embrace our technology partners. Last, yet most important, we must change how we regulate and finance the industry."

Dean describes his efforts to establish a decarbonized energy network, to experiment with microgrids that can monitor energy flows to create two-way flows between company and customer, and to empower the entire energy supply chain, including system operators, generators, distributors, and customers. Customers, he correctly notes, want more control over how and when they use energy. He's not fighting this trend. Why? "Because in the end, it will drive a more sustainable long-term model."

Ultimately, Dean's vision is to "redefine utilities as a kind of smartphone for energy distribution, with energy generators, service providers, and technology partners delivering a range of energy-solution apps."

Dean admits he doesn't have all the answers yet. But he does know he "must put customers in charge, embrace technology partners, and see real change in how the industry is financed . . . in order to kill our twentieth-century infrastructure paradigm for one that works in the twenty-first century and beyond."

What do Jim, Dean, and most in the energy sector understand? That they must act now, and that they must co-create the context in which energy decisions will be made with numerous—

and even some unlikely—partners, and that they must relinquish control to create an optimum, enduring, and sustainable outcome.

Inviting everyone to provide energy to the grid and giving customers a voice in designing and meeting their energy requirements is relinquishing control to preserve power in practice.

However, at least for now, there are more examples of leaders succumbing to the fear of losing power by aggressively seeking to exert greater control.

• • •

It was May of 2003, and General Dempsey was about to depart Riyadh, Saudi Arabia, where he was serving as the program manager of the Saudi Arabian National Guard Modernization Program and adviser to Crown Prince Abdullah bin Abdul-Aziz. He was headed to Baghdad to become commander of the U.S. Army First Armored Division, which had recently been assigned responsibility for securing the Iraqi capital. Crown Prince Abdullah had been good to General Dempsey's group of several hundred soldiers and civilians, who were working in several locations in the kingdom to help him modernize his National Guard. General Dempsey made sure to pay the crown prince a courtesy visit before leaving the area; while protocol matters in most countries across the globe, it matters especially in monarchies.

General Dempsey's car turned into the crown prince's palace. It was heavily guarded, but Dempsey had been there before, and the guards rendered a crisp salute as his car drove through the security checkpoint. The palace grounds were an impressive combination of polished marble and verdant gardens, a beautiful sight to take in while traversing the hundred-yard driveway. And a stark contrast to life outside the palace.

Crown Prince Abdullah was aware of the contrast and had proven himself both an astute reformer and a compassionate leader. He was destined to be the next king, and there was general enthusiasm for the moment that day would arrive. It wouldn't be long.

The tires of Dempsey's armored sedan squealed on the marble driveway as they turned slowly toward the dismount point in front of the palace. The adviser to the crown prince greeted him warmly as he stepped out of the car. The adviser spoke perfect English and had been a very helpful interlocutor for Dempsey over the past two years.

"Good morning, Adil," he said, extending his hand in greeting.

"Good morning, General," Adil responded. "The crown prince is eager to see you. It will be just a few minutes, as some local farmers have come to ask his assistance, and they are in with His Royal Highness right now."

"I understand, Adil. No worries," Dempsey replied in Arabic. Adil smiled.

In the kingdom that was Saudi Arabia, anyone could, and many often did, directly petition the royal family for assistance. The relationship between the royal family and the population was what held the country together. It was a tenuous relationship at times, strained by the intersection of religious conservatism and modernity, but they made it work. For now, at least, Dempsey thought.

In any case, General Dempsey was aware that it could be minutes or hours before he would have his audience with the crown prince. He had learned quickly that patience and courtesy were indispensable attributes for those working in Saudi Arabia. A servant carrying a pot of Arabic coffee approached. It was bitter to the taste but on most occasions a welcome part of the ritual. Tea would come next. Then water or juice. If Dempsey was there long enough, the cycle would repeat.

"Thank you," he said, again in Arabic. The servant smiled, but there was never any exchange with these Bedouins who loyally served the crown prince.

General Dempsey's escort sat down beside him.

"How's your family?" he asked. This too was part of the ritual: reinforce the relationship before business.

"Very well. Thanks for asking, Adil. And how about yours?"

For the next fifteen minutes the pair discussed events outside the kingdom. Al Qaeda, Iraq, Egypt, Israel, the Palestinians, Iran. Especially Iran. Iran had supplanted Israel as the topic of greatest interest.

Adil excused himself. General Dempsey sat looking around the expansive waiting room. It was about the size of a basketball court and was adorned with several beautifully embroidered and elaborately framed verses from the Koran. There was also a single modestly sized portrait: King Abdulaziz, the founder of the Kingdom of Saudi Arabia. Otherwise there were no images or statuary here. That would have been contrary to the tenets of Islam. The single silk rug—probably woven in Iran—that covered all but a few feet on each side of the room must have been unimaginably expensive. There were at least a hundred beautifully upholstered chairs around the room.

At certain times of the year, this room would be filled with well-wishers and petitioners. They would come and go throughout the evening, and each time a member of the royal family entered the room, everyone would stand and shuffle to new positions based on the "rank" of the newcomer relative to those already in the room. Dempsey could never figure out how they kept track of it all and was glad that today he would not be competing much longer for the crown prince's attention. Adil returned.

"The crown prince will see you now," he said. "Please follow me."

It was only a short walk to the room where the crown prince awaited General Dempsey's arrival. The room was a smaller, more intimate version of the waiting room.

The crown prince stood and approached Dempsey, who

greeted him in Arabic and kissed him on both cheeks. The crown prince took his hand, guiding him to two armchairs at the front of the room. Between the armchairs was a straight-backed chair. Adil would sit there to translate.

"How is my general?" the crown prince asked.

"I'm well, Your Royal Highness. And how are you?"

Relationship before business. Legend has it that an American general visiting from Washington once looked at his watch several times during a visit, and the crown prince was highly insulted. General Dempsey never wore a watch while serving in the kingdom.

Coffee, tea, fruit juice. The crown prince was ready to get to the subject of the visit.

"General, I'm told that you will be leaving us. We are sorry to see you leave. You have been an honest adviser and have helped us prepare our National Guard for an uncertain future. Thank you very much."

Dempsey's turn.

"Your Royal Highness, it has been my honor to serve in the kingdom with the National Guard. They benefit greatly from your support, and the relationship between our Army and your National Guard has never been stronger."

"General, I know your next duty will be in Iraq. I wish you success. It will be a very difficult mission. You can be sure that the Iranians will try to disrupt your efforts."

"Yes, sir. I'm sure there will be many who will not want us to succeed. Do you have any advice for me?" Dempsey asked.

The crown prince paused, leaning toward Dempsey and looking at him closely.

"Be careful not to alter the face of Islam," he said somberly.

It would be a few months before Dempsey understood what he meant.

General Dempsey knew that the courtesy call was almost

over. A photographer entered the room, and the interpreter rose from his chair. He wanted to learn more, but it was time to go. Dempsey stood up. A picture, a handshake, a final expression of appreciation, and Dempsey's time in Saudi Arabia was at an end.

General Dempsey has often reflected on the moment the crown prince urged him to be careful not to alter the face of Islam. For several hundred years the Sunni sect of Islam has dominated the Middle East. With the demise of dictators and monarchs, competition erupted: majorities and minorities, conservatives and moderates, tribes and newly empowered politicians, expatriates, and indigenous. But the competition between Sunni and Shia for the soul of Islam fuels the violence that persists today in the Middle East.

The invasion of Iraq in 2003 didn't "alter the face of Islam," but in its attempt to introduce democratic principles to the region, it did alter the balance of power between Sunni and Shia. And as these two sects of Islam began to seek advantage over each other and to compete for control of Iraq, they would thrust the region into decades of conflict.

• • •

The theater at Camp Lejeune was full. It was the spring of 2015, and six hundred Marines had been invited—or more likely marched—to the theater for a town hall meeting with the Chairman of the Joint Chiefs of Staff. General Dempsey always appreciated the opportunity to meet servicemen and servicewomen and their families as he traveled around the country.

These personal contacts had become even more important as social media and 24/7 news coverage had inundated young servicemen and servicewomen and their families as they prepared for a very uncertain and dangerous future. He could often tell from their questions where they were getting their "news."

This day's group seemed most interested in recent studies on retirement reform and in the ongoing debate about opening combat assignments to women. They were respectful but direct, which Dempsey appreciated.

From the back of the theater, a Marine gunnery sergeant asked what Dempsey intended to do about ISIS. The Marine reminded him that the U.S. military had paid a heavy price in the Middle East in 1991 during Operation Desert Storm, in 2003 in Operation Iraqi Freedom, and again in 2007 during the surge. He said that in his judgment it had been a mistake to withdraw from Iraq in 2011, and he suggested that the military should reverse that decision, deploy a ground force large enough to finish off ISIS quickly, and then bring them home. Heads nodded in agreement.

"That's a great question, Gunny," Dempsey responded. "You've obviously got some history in the region. Thanks for your service over there. I'd like to share a perspective about what's going on with ISIS right now and see what you think of it."

"Hoorah, sir," he responded. (That's Marine-speak for "Go right ahead, sir.")

"ISIS is just the latest manifestation of much deeper issues confronting the region," Dempsey began. "The region is rife with corruption, ineffective governance, religious hostility, and economic instability. Unless and until these issues are addressed, military success won't matter. ISIS could disappear tomorrow, and a new group with a new name and a new extremist ideology would appear to take its place."

"So what do we do, sir?" asked the gunnery sergeant. "We can't just do nothing."

"I agree with you, Gunny. But let me come at this from another direction for a minute." Dempsey was about to abruptly change topics. "Did you ever play golf?"

He nodded yes.

"Well, suppose I get up on the first tee, take a stance, check my grip, address the ball, swing, and hook it into the woods a hundred yards down the fairway. Then on the second tee, I take up the same stance, place my hands in the same grip, address the ball the same way, swing, and hook it into the woods a hundred yards down the fairway. Then on the third tee I do exactly the same things with exactly the same result. Should I go to the fourth tee thinking that I'm going to do everything the way I did it on the previous three holes? Of course not. That would be silly. Don't get me wrong, I've actually done that in golf."

The audience laughed.

"But that's not what we should be doing in Iraq. Look, we're on our fourth try in Iraq. Each of the previous three times we've made a commitment in Iraq, we've rolled in heavy, taken control, reduced the levels of violence, imposed order on the political and economic systems, and then given it all back to the Iraqis. And each time they have proven unequal to the task. You can argue that we didn't do enough to get them ready. I argue that we did too much and removed the incentive for them to be ready."

"What's going to be different this time, sir?" came a question from a Marine in the front row.

"This time we don't take control," Dempsey replied. "This time we go in to support—enough to do what we want to do, but not so much that they get the impression we're making this primarily our fight. This time we provide a limited number of resources that they simply don't have: air power, intelligence, logistics, and training. We place enough of our own direct-strike capability in country to hit targets that could directly threaten our personnel and facilities or our homeland. But this time we make it clear that we're there to support *their* campaign plan. We advise; they decide. It will take longer, and progress will be uneven, but it will be theirs. Simultaneously, we help them plan for success, for the day ISIS is defeated, and we make it clear that our support depends on them working together."

"Makes sense," said the gunnery sergeant. "Will it work?"

"I honestly don't know, Gunny," Dempsey replied. "But I do know that doing it the same way we did it before won't work. We'll give them another chance and show them what being included in determining the outcome really looks like. If we're patient, I do think it will work."

Dempsey has long considered the period between his visit to the crown prince in Riyadh in 2003 and his visit to the Marines at Camp Lejeune in 2015 and what it means for the future. The issues tearing the Middle East apart will not be resolved for a generation. Moreover, the issues are not confined to the Middle East. They are prevalent in an "arc of instability" that stretches from Afghanistan in the east to Nigeria in the west. The cost of unilaterally controlling matters in this arc of instability for twenty years would be unimaginable. But there is an answer, and it is an answer based on the principle of radical inclusion. We should counter radical extremism with radical inclusion.

The instability in the Middle East, South Asia, and North Africa affects us, our allies, and our partners. Terrorism, migration, arms trafficking, and drugs flow through ungoverned or poorly governed space, but they don't stop there. They threaten us and our allies. They relentlessly assault our values and our sense of well-being.

Those responsible for this instability—the loosely affiliated radical Islamist groups who profess exclusion and who practice violent religious extremism across the region—can be defeated only by a broad and inclusive coalition, a coalition with the capability, the resources, and the staying power to collaborate on the whole problem: security, governance, reconstruction, economic development, and humanitarian relief.

Against this enemy, we should use military force only if

we are willing to complement it with the use of the other instruments of our national power. That should also be the "price of admission" to the coalition. Progress in the campaign should be measured less in terms of enemies killed and cities liberated and more in terms of functioning institutions, the restoration of basic goods and services, and the completion of reconstruction projects.

Such a coalition must be "owned" by those countries in the region that have both the most to lose and the most to gain by the outcome. Otherwise, the outcomes will simply not endure.

Countries outside the region—including the United States—must be willing to relinquish control at times and in places in the interest of generating a genuine sense of belonging, ownership, and accountability among those engaged in this conflict.

• • •

Relinquishing control is about partnering with like-minded individuals, teams, and organizations to solve problems in ways that will endure. It is about solving problems and conserving power at a cost that is sustainable for us and our organizations. It is not about being liberal or progressive, or being inclusive for the sake of being egalitarian. Leaders must learn to relinquish control in order to solve problems effectively and efficiently, and to keep those problems solved in the long term. By relinquishing control, we preserve and enhance our power.

• • •

As General Dempsey's car turned off Massachusetts Avenue in northwest Washington and into the British embassy, the security guard greeted him with a broad smile: "Good to see you again, General, and good on you! Enjoy the evening. Please pull forward and park just there in the roundabout. It's just a short walk from there to the residence."

Dempsey had been to the British ambassador's residence a half dozen times in the past five years, usually to meet a visiting British dignitary. On one memorable occasion, Prince Charles was in town to support a charitable event for U.S. and British soldiers wounded in the wars in Iraq and Afghanistan. Dempsey spoke just before the prince, and to lighten the moment he sang a verse of an Irish ballad. Not to be outdone, and to the utter astonishment of the other British dignitaries in the room, Prince Charles ended his remarks with a verse from *The Pirates of Penzance*. It was good fun for a good cause.

Tonight would be good fun too. It was October 2016 and Dempsey was there to be invested as a Knight of the British Empire, the first U.S. military officer to be so honored in the last twelve years and one of only twenty-six U.S. military officers ever accorded the honor.

The British ambassador's residence is one of the most beautiful and impressive buildings in a city full of beautiful and impressive buildings. Opened in 1928, its marbled floors, sturdy Ionic columns, gilded artwork, and carefully manicured English garden are a journey back in time.

Dempsey was escorted to the library to await the ceremony. The titles on its shelves were an impressive sampling of England's rich literary history. Years earlier Dempsey had read and even taught many of these books. A working knowledge of literature had always helped him find metaphors to understand and describe the complexities of national security. But he wouldn't be quoting English literature to his English hosts tonight. Tonight was about celebrating common values, shared commitments, and collaboration on complex problems.

About seventy-five of Dempsey's family and closest friends were present. The news for the past month or more had been consistently unsettling and often divisive. His British colleagues were understandably anxious about how the two countries' relationship would evolve. Dempsey wanted to say something meaningful and reassuring.

At the appointed time he was escorted from the library and into the room where the ceremony would take place. He smiled at the front row of guests, where his wife, his three children, and six of his nine grandchildren were sitting.

In the few moments before the ambassador entered the room, Dempsey glanced above the large fireplace on one side of the room to a portrait of Queen Elizabeth I. Directly across on the other side of the room was a portrait of Queen Elizabeth II. Though more than four hundred years apart, each of them faced strikingly similar challenges and deftly guided England through war and peace, through great shifts in power, and through dramatic societal change. Something, some instinct, made them equal to their times. "We must be equal to our time," Dempsey thought.

The room rose as one when the ambassador entered the room. He summoned Dempsey to his side. His remarks were extensive and complimentary. As the ambassador spoke, Dempsey found himself reflecting on what he'd learned about America's relationship with the British and what he had done with the knowledge.

From 1941 to 1948, the Combined Chiefs of Staff of the United States and the United Kingdom met annually in Washington and in London, initially to chart the course of the war and subsequently to collaboratively plan for the security of postwar Europe. The Combined Chiefs included the senior military officer of each country with his chiefs of Army, Navy, and Marines. Their insights, strategies, and advice were provided to the president of the United States and the prime minister of Great Britain for consideration in making important policy and resource decisions.

The 1947 Combined Chiefs meeting was particularly important. It was held in Roosevelt Hall at Fort McNair in Washington DC. The war in Europe and the war in the Pacific had been over for more than a year, and the military arsenals of both the United States and the United Kingdom were being dismantled. Defense budgets in each country were being redirected to economic priorities. Faced with declining resources and increasing requirements, the Combined Chiefs met to determine how they could better collaborate on managing the mutual national security risks they identified.

In late 2012 Dempsey had met his British counterpart—Chief of Defence Staff General Sir David Richards—in London to discuss the state of their two countries' armed forces. They both faced declining resources after a decade of war in Iraq and Afghanistan, and they both assessed security in Europe and in the Pacific as trending downward. Sir David suggested that they take a page from their shared history and revive the Combined Chiefs of Staff meeting. Dempsey agreed and offered to host the first event in Washington DC in the summer of 2013. They decided to model their meeting on the 1947 meeting.

"Her Majesty the Queen is pleased to confer on this great friend of England the title of Honorary Knight of the Most Excellent Order of the British Empire," the ambassador concluded.

Dempsey snapped back to the present.

He began his remarks by asking the ambassador to express his deep appreciation and humility to Her Majesty the Queen for this great honor. He told the ambassador that he accepted the award on behalf of the thousands of U.S. soldiers, sailors, airmen, and Marines who had served and continued to serve in peace and in war alongside the men and women of Britain's Defence Forces. "For the past forty years, wherever and whenever I've served, Britain's sons and daughters have been at my side," Dempsey said.

"I'd like to elaborate on the importance of the Combined Chiefs of Staff Strategy meetings," he told the assembled guests, "but I want to begin by telling my grandchildren that this award I've received tonight is about friendship, respect, and trust. It's about two countries who believe in each other and who share the same values. What I want my grandchildren to remember from tonight is that we get through life by choosing our friends carefully, working with them on the hardest problems, and trusting them.

"In 2013 the Combined Chiefs of Staff of the U.S. and UK met in the same room in the same building as our predecessors in 1947. We sat in the same seats and even took a black and-white group photograph with each of us standing where our predecessors had stood for their group photograph. We met to share our assessments of global security, to discuss our resource challenges, and to determine if we could do more together than we could do separately. We challenged ourselves to consider becoming not just more collaborative and interoperable but interdependent in select areas. Separately we knew we couldn't do more with less. Together we thought we might.

"The meeting played out in the context of a resurgent Russia, an assertive China, an aggressive North Korea, an insidious Iran, and the reality of a generational and persistent conflict with violent extremist groups from Afghanistan to Nigeria.

"We succeeded in finding areas where we could each recommend relinquishing some control in order to achieve interdependence and a better outcome. We wrote our report. I presented a copy to our president; General Sir David presented a copy to his prime minister. They validated our recommendations. We made a commitment to have working groups track our progress toward interdependence and to meet again the next year in London.

"This award tonight is symbolic of what we have and must continue to learn from this experience. That is, the key to dealing with life's complexity, uncertainty, and adversity is to find someone you trust . . . and trust them."

It takes trust to relinquish control, but with trust anything is possible; without trust, almost nothing.

• • •

Leaders in the new environment must understand that relinquishing control is a matter of necessity. In a world where control is too costly, where the answers rarely lie with us and often lie with our people, and where the environment is adapting more quickly than we can react, we must relinquish control for self-preservation; to preserve our positions as leaders and to build and sustain the power of our organizations, we have no option but to let go of control.

Real power, the kind of power that yields optimum, enduring, and affordable outcomes, is not a liability. But in order to build and sustain that kind of power, leaders need to develop the instinct for seeking opportunities to share control.

Simply put, relinquishing control yields better, longer-lasting solutions that will preserve and enhance your power as a leader and your power as an organization. Those who do not learn to relinquish control will suffer costly effects. As our environment changes and adapts, these effects have the potential to increase exponentially and lead to catastrophe for individuals, teams, and organizations.

Leaders must understand, however, that relinquishing control works only when there is an ethos in place that supports it. The workforce or members of the team must feel a genuine commitment to the organization and its vision if we are to trust our subordinates to think and act appropriately when afforded the opportunity to take more powerful roles within the organization. Relinquishing control must be accompanied by a deliberate effort to follow through with the previous five principles.

Relinquishing control to build and sustain power feels counterintuitive, but in fact it has less to do with a leader losing power and more to do with how an organization shares knowledge and builds trust.

But how can we be sure we let go of enough power to be effective, but not so much that we lose it all? How can leaders learn to go against their natural instincts to seize control when they feel it slipping away?

There are instincts that every leader must develop in order to be successful in his mission to learn to relinquish control. It is through these instincts that leaders find the necessary trust in their team members, discover a method to utilize the ideas and knowledge that exist throughout the organization, and build and sustain the power of the organization not through control but by radical inclusion.

CHAPTER 12: **THE LEADERSHIP**
INSTINCTS: LISTEN, AMPLIFY, INCLUDE

Kansas can be quite hot in June, and on this particular day it was exceeding expectations. Major Dempsey had just finished his studies at the Army's midcareer school at Fort Leavenworth, Kansas, and this was the graduation ceremony. Outside, on metal folding chairs, in wool uniforms, in the blazing sun. *Nice,* he thought.

His mind was mostly on the task ahead: packing up his family and heading to Germany for his next assignment as a tank battalion executive officer. The transition would be tough on Deanie and the kids, he knew, but they would eventually turn it into an adventure.

Dempsey was only vaguely aware that the guest speaker for the ceremony was being introduced, but it was the four-star commander of U.S. Army Europe, so he figured he'd better pay attention.

General Glenn Otis took the podium and congratulated the graduating class. He told the thousand men and women before him about the state of the Army in Europe and about the importance of the mission as part of our nation's commitment to NATO. Then he said he wanted the graduates to remember just one thing from his remarks that day. He took a 3x5 card from his breast pocket.

"I carry this card with me at all times," he said, "to remind me about the most important attribute of a leader. The card reads 'When is the last time you allowed a subordinate to change your mind about something?' I want you to remember this as you leave here today and rejoin the regular Army: be a good listener."

General Otis made an impression on Dempsey that day. From then on, he carried a similar reminder to himself about being a good listener.

As he progressed in his own career, Dempsey added two other attributes that he considered essential in a leader: understanding how to amplify and developing a genuine instinct to be inclusive.

He describes the interaction of the three instincts this way:

Listen to learn. Listen to make it clear to those who follow that you value their insights, their judgments, and their advice. Listen to understand the organization and to become mindful of opportunities and vulnerabilities. Listen because it is most often "weak signals" that portend success or failure.

Amplify to establish expectations. Amplify the best ideas, the best recommendations, the best practices, and do so in a manner that encourages teamwork at every level of the organization. Amplify the organization's values to strengthen the inner voice that reminds us what's right, a voice that can sometimes be drowned out by digital echoes. Amplify because the best leaders establish a drumbeat of emphasis on values within their organization. Amplify because everyone benefits when there is a common vocabulary about what's expected of them.

Include to empower. Go wide and deep in including members of the organization to share knowledge, to create a common understanding of problems, and to encourage ownership of solutions. Include to inspire loyalty. Include as the first step in developing a climate of trust. Include because if you don't, who will?

• • •

Leaders operating under the leadership theory described in this book will find it difficult to succeed without developing an instinct for listening. Those who are frequently extrapolating and pontificating are rarely able to truly empower those around them and open the lines of communication in the ways this book's principles have taught. Leaders must understand that the instinct to listen is an art, a skill, and a system that must be employed in order build a team ethos, embrace a bias for action, and relinquish control. So how do we listen—not only leaders but organizations as a whole?

Opportunities to listen are all around us: personal interactions, structured and unstructured meetings, walking the halls, social media, town hall meetings, conversations in the elevator. Everywhere and anywhere are opportunities to listen.

The more willing we are to seek these opportunities and capitalize on them, the more likely we are to continue to develop the instinct and become stronger listeners as people and as teams. We must discover efficient, realistic ways to listen to members of our organizations at every level so that we may (a) better understand the problems our people are facing, (b) recognize the potential solutions our team members have thought of, and (c) provide our team members with their own opportunities to lead.

General Dempsey remembers one of his first meetings with the president. He can't recall the topic, but he remembers vividly how focused he was on listening to the president's words and working to understand not only their meaning but their context. He soaked in the words, volume, facial expression, eye contact, and body language. If Dempsey was to be his adviser for the next four years, he needed to know how this man thought and communicated.

What if we listened more intently and worked harder to understand what others were trying to communicate? Doing so would improve our relationships and build the trust necessary to lead more effectively.

When General Dempsey and the Joint Chiefs were tasked to develop a plan to train and educate the force before the military rescinded the "don't ask, don't tell" policy, they immediately sent out several key military and civilian leaders on a "listening tour." Their mandate was to find out what the men and women across the armed forces—active and reserve—were thinking, were saying, and were feeling. The Joint Chiefs had decided that only when they had this information would they begin to formulate a plan and a time line for rescinding the policy.

When a leader listens, he has the opportunity to find answers to the problems the organization faces. He empowers his team members to be an active part of the decision-making process, thus cultivating a sense of belonging. The leader can take this a step further by not only listening for innovative solutions but also amplifying those successes throughout the organization.

By amplifying the successful ideas and solutions created by members of our teams, leaders show how relinquishing control, empowering the team, and listening benefit the organization as a whole. They advance the mission of the organization by making positive examples of the kinds of ideas and actions that achieve results necessary for optimum, enduring, and sustainable success.

Good leaders share credit and accept blame. Good leaders don't simply proclaim an interest in initiative and innovation but articulate how much risk they are willing to take to enable initiative and innovation. They define the "white lines" on the road they expect their subordinates to travel. Even more important than establishing limits, they champion success.

General Dempsey absolutely embraced the differences among the armed services during his time as Chairman of the Joint Chiefs. He applauded their individual cultures and traditions while at the same time working diligently to integrate them into the broader missions of the Joint Force. He valued diverse thinking from senior military leaders who saw America's security, and its vulnerabilities and opportunities, through different lenses. There was always a bit of friction as this group of very senior, very experienced leaders expressed themselves during weekly meetings, but he saw it as his job—as the senior leader among them—to ensure that it was *creative friction*.

Not surprisingly, there were times when one service or another would outperform the others. In those times, Dempsey would gather the Service Chiefs to discuss the issues. He would amplify successes and encourage these highly competitive and accomplished senior leaders to align their efforts. The more they listened to one another, the more they learned from one another, and the more likely it became that they would amplify one another's efforts.

Generally, when facing a problem, the Joint Chiefs of Staff would together establish objectives for solving it collectively. Then, with the authorities inherent within the services, each service would set about the task of accomplishing those objectives. There were plenty of opportunities to compare outcomes. In one six-month period of 2014, General Dempsey recalls reviewing plans for care of the wounded, efforts to reduce suicide, prevention of sexual assault, and integration of women into jobs previously closed to them. Each of these issues, and many more, posed challenges of implementation. In resolving these challenges, the

Joint Chiefs never allowed themselves to throw up the "shield" of differences among the services. They amplified what they could learn from one another.

When a leader amplifies the successes of the members of his organization at all levels of responsibility, he provides more than a teaching moment to his team about what success looks like. It is not only a "pat on the back" for the individual whose success is amplified. It's a memory, and it's one that matters. It's an action taken to further the mission of the team. It has helped to reinforce a sense of belonging and demonstrate the leader's willingness to relinquish control.

All of these principles and instincts are what this new leadership theory deems necessary for companies and countries to thrive in the new environment. Through constant reinforcement of these principles and ongoing development of these instincts, leaders can develop teams and organizations that will build and sustain their power not through control but by radical inclusion.

PART 4

IN INCLUSION WE TRUST

CHAPTER 13: **TRUST EARNED**
EARLY AND OFTEN

Digital Echoes Are Loud; Trust Lowers the Volume

On June 5, 1974, General Dempsey was commissioned as a second lieutenant in the U.S. Army following his graduation from West Point. As part of the ritual of commissioning, each new officer selects an enlisted soldier to render the "first salute." Most often, it is someone who has been an important part of the new officer's development. Dempsey chose Sergeant Major Bernie Henderson.

Bernie Henderson was the senior armor noncommissioned officer in the Department of Military Instruction. Because Dempsey had known since his sophomore year that he wanted to become an armor officer, Henderson had become a mentor to him.

Sergeant Major Henderson was a superb leader. A Vietnam veteran with several decades of military experience, he was a great listener, a patient teacher, and a man of uncompromising principles. Though Dempsey was a young man not yet twenty-one years old when he first met the sergeant major, Henderson treated him with genuine respect. He also made sure Dempsey understood the important advisory role of the noncommissioned officer in our Army.

As Dempsey's oath of commissioning was read and his mother and father pinned on his second lieutenant insignia, he turned to see Sergeant Major Henderson approaching from his right.

Henderson snapped off a crisp salute and proclaimed, "Welcome to the regular Army, Lieutenant Dempsey!" As is the custom, Dempsey returned his salute and thanked him for his part in Dempsey's becoming an officer.

In return for the "first salute," officers are expected to give the noncommissioned officer a silver dollar. In 1974, silver dollars had become scarce, so most of Dempsey's classmates had elected to hand the noncommissioned officer a signed dollar bill instead.

Dempsey reached in his pocket and felt around for the dollar bill he had placed there an hour earlier. He found it and handed it to Sergeant Major Henderson. Henderson smiled and said, "I'll send this back to you when you become a general." Dempsey chuckled and told him that if that was the case, he'd never see that dollar again. Henderson told him not to worry about making general but simply to earn the trust of his soldiers, as Dempsey had earned his trust. It was an emotional moment as Henderson turned and walked away.

To his great regret, Dempsey lost track of Henderson. He would hear of him from time to time, but most of Dempsey's early career was spent in Germany, and Henderson had retired in Maryland.

The years passed, and in 2001 Dempsey became a brigadier general. The Chairman of the Joint Chiefs of Staff, General Hugh Shelton, presided over a nice ceremony in the Pentagon. For just a brief moment, as the ceremony concluded and Dempsey was announced as Brigadier General Martin Dempsey, he thought of Sergeant Major Henderson's prediction.

In June 2014 Dempsey reached forty years of commissioned service in the Army. His classmates were planning a reunion for the fall, so the exact day passed without fanfare. But later in June, a package arrived at Dempsey's quarters. He was more than surprised to see on the return address that it was sent by one Sergeant Major (Retired) Bernie Henderson. Inside the package was a framed one-dollar bill with Dempsey's signature on it. The note that accompanied it said, "I told you I would return this to you when you made General. Sorry it took so long. Bernie Henderson."

It brought Dempsey to tears. That framed dollar now sits on his desk to remind him of how one person's trust in another can be so empowering.

Nine months before Dempsey was to retire as Chairman of the Joint Chiefs of Staff, in January 2015, he was told that Vice President Biden, who was scheduled to give the commencement address at West Point that year, wanted to offer that honor to him. This was unusual—commencement addresses at the four service academies are normally given by the president, the vice president, the secretary of defense, and the service secretaries—but Dempsey immediately accepted and thanked the vice president. It was a very nice gesture by a very thoughtful leader.

Of course, once Dempsey accepted the offer, he began to feel anxious about the task. Like many college graduates, he couldn't even remember who had given the commencement address at his graduation. He wanted to leave these graduates something to remember.

January and February ticked by, and Dempsey still hadn't decided how he would approach the speech. He was rarely nervous about public speaking; this was the exception.

One evening in early March, Dempsey walked past the

bookcase where Bernie Henderson's framed one-dollar bill was displayed. In that moment, he knew what he would do. The next day, he asked Deanie for $1,100. Dempsey almost never carried more cash than he needed for an occasional haircut, so she asked what it was for. He told her.

As he walked into Michie Stadium in May 2015 for West Point's graduation ceremony, his heart was racing. Just over a thousand eager seniors turned to watch their fellow West Pointer—a four-star general and Chairman of the Joint Chiefs of Staff—mount the stage. It was to these young men and women that Dempsey would soon turn over the reins of America's armed forces when his time was done.

After the introductions and invocations, it was Dempsey's turn to speak. He warmed them up with a little "graduation karaoke," including a verse of Sinatra's "New York, New York." And then, in the culmination of a twelve-minute commencement address, he told them that all they needed to remember about his time with them on that day were these three words: "I trust you."

As they proudly marched across the stage to receive their diplomas, Dempsey handed each of them a crisp, new one-dollar bill. It probably wasn't until they had returned to their seats that they noticed he had signed each bill.

Sergeant Major Henderson would have approved.

Henderson knew, Dempsey learned, and these new officers would soon find out that the essence of leadership is building trust.

• • •

With this book we provide leaders with a theory to help them prevail in what has become a very challenging leadership environment: a theory that calls upon us to emphasize where we converge, not where we diverge, to emphasize inclusion. Through the principles and instincts provided here, leaders will develop a preference for inclusion over power. As we've made clear, we advocate inclusion because of its pragmatic advantages.

Inclusion leads to greater knowledge for leaders and organizations about the nature of the problems we face and the ways in which we may solve them. We strongly believe that inclusion yields better outcomes for countries, more affordable outcomes for companies, and more enduring outcomes for military operations.

Though he ended up Chairman of the Joint Chiefs of Staff with an instinct for inclusion, General Dempsey says that his instinct was developed long before, in Central Europe, in the Mojave Desert, and in the Middle East.

The platoon is a young Army officer's first leadership test. In 1974 twenty-two-year-old Dempsey's platoon of forty-five soldiers was tasked with patrolling the border between West Germany and Czechoslovakia. Though it's just a distant memory now, Dempsey recalls that border as the line of demarcation between the Warsaw Pact (led by the Soviet Union) and the North Atlantic Treaty Organization (led by the United States). The platoon patrolled mounted in jeeps and in armored vehicles. They lived in austere, remote border camps filled with Quonset huts surrounded by chain-link fence and barbed wire. Their tour of duty was for thirty days at a time, two or three times a year. The rest of the year they trained for the mission at their kaserne some sixty kilometers to the west.

Generally groups of two or three vehicles with six to eight soldiers would patrol around the clock over a linear distance of seven to ten kilometers. In the days before readily available satellite imagery and full-motion video feeds from remotely piloted aircraft, they were the eyes and ears of senior military officers and civilian officials in places like Nuremberg, Frankfurt, and Bonn.

In such circumstances, individuals learn to trust one another. No one could possibly be everywhere and see everything, and so they relied on one another to understand the mission, to be vigilant, to be responsive in reporting back on events during the patrol, and to adapt when circumstances changed. In these circumstances, everyone had to contribute, everyone had to be included.

Initially, Dempsey had concluded that he could rely on some but not all of the forty-five soldiers under his command. There were significant drug and racial problems in the Army in 1974, and Dempsey's platoon was no exception. When he first met the platoon, they were fragmented by race, divided into those who used drugs and those who didn't, those who liked one kind of music and those who preferred another—almost any excuse to be exclusionary.

General Dempsey doesn't recall the exact day when he decided that developing and exhibiting an instinct for inclusion was the only way to bring the unit together and, in so doing, accomplish the mission. It might have happened on a makeshift basketball court, or around a foosball table in the mess hall, or in the motor pool while struggling to figure out how to change impossibly heavy sections of track on an armored vehicle in a foot of mud. However it happened, it worked. Dempsey got those forty-five soldiers to work together on something, and then on something else, and eventually on everything. And he did it by making sure that he valued the contributions of each of them, as individuals first and then as part of the team.

Some of them eventually got thrown out of the Army. A few for repeated drug offenses. One or two for multiple acts of disobedience or absence. One for a bar fight back near their home station. But not for how they interacted with the team. When Dempsey had them together, focused on some common purpose and understanding that they all mattered, they were a very special group. It was with this group that Dempsey first recognized the power of inclusion.

In October 1997, Dempsey took his cavalry regiment to the Mojave Desert to be tested. They were 5,200 strong. Like his cavalry platoon of 1974, they were the eyes and ears of more senior officers: in this case the leaders of an armored corps that, when fully arrayed on the battlefield, numbered more than 50,000. The cavalry regiment is usually "out front" harvesting information, sometimes fighting for information, and always shaping the battlefield for the remainder of the corps as it moves behind them.

The test in the Mojave Desert was a hard one, against a world-class opposing force on its "home court," in remarkably harsh desert conditions. The Army wanted "the scrimmage to be harder than the game," and the Mojave Desert was the perfect place for that. To accomplish its mission, the cavalry regiment spread out. (It can operate thirty to fifty kilometers across in an advance or stretch a hundred kilometers along a linear boundary in a defense.)

The cavalry regiment is an interesting organizational design because it combines most of the Army's occupational specialties into a single organization: scouts to find the enemy, tankers to destroy it at short range, artillerymen to suppress it at long distance, aviators to dominate from the air, engineers to improve mobility, air defenders to protect the skies above, and logisticians to keep supplies and equipment at the ready.

In such an organization, parochialisms are natural. Soldiers in each specialty argue that their contribution is the most indispensable. Some of the competition is healthy and productive; some can be unproductive. The challenge is to convince 5,200 soldiers that together they can be greater than the sum of their individual parts—the familiar leadership challenge of developing a sense of inclusion.

In this case, the answer was to focus on the core mission. Dempsey found a memorable way of describing it and then frequently reinforced the message. He told the men and women of the regiment and their leaders, "We are all scouts." For the year preceding the test in the desert, he visited training ranges, motor pools, dining facilities, and barracks. At each stop Dempsey asked soldiers, "What do you do in this regiment?" Initially they would reply, "I'm a mechanic" or "I'm a cook" or "I'm a clerk." "Wrong!" Dempsey would reply. "You're a scout." And then he would explain why.

Whether on the front lines or in the rear, whether driving a tank or a fuel truck, whether ensuring communications or food supply, whether a private or a colonel, they all became scouts. Everyone became aware, vigilant, and committed to creating a shared understanding of what was happening on the battlefield: 5,200 sets of eyes and ears. Everyone included, everyone contributing. It worked. They passed the test. There were other keys to their success, but developing a sense of inclusion was the necessary start to it all.

Six years later, Dempsey found himself in command of the Army's First Armored Division with 32,000 soldiers in Baghdad. The stakes and the risks were higher but the leadership challenge the same.

The U.S. Army and its sister services are the preeminent leader-development institutions in the land. They have to be. They train centralized but operate decentralized. They face opponents who don't just want to gain an advantage over them but want to drive them from the battlefield. Opponents who are determined and who are adaptable.

The soldiers must trust one another. Soldiers will willingly put themselves in harm's way only if they trust the man or woman to their left and right, the medic who accompanies them, the pilots who fly over them, and the leaders who direct them. Absent trust, a military unit can accomplish little; with it, the unit can accomplish almost anything.

Trust is built over time. It begins with inclusion. When

Dempsey arrived in Baghdad, what had changed since his days patrolling the border in Germany was the degree of decentralization and the transparency that existed in units big and small. In some ways, Dempsey says, these things make inclusion easier. In other ways they make it harder.

Baghdad is a city of just over seven hundred square kilometers, physically divided by a river but divided far more fundamentally by ethnic, tribal, and religious rivalries. The task for Dempsey and his 32,000 soldiers was to "establish a safe and secure environment" in which Iraq's fledgling political leaders could reestablish control of their capital city and country. That task remains even today a work in progress, but not for lack of effort and sacrifice by America's men and women in uniform.

Based on Baghdad's ethnic and religious "fault lines," the city was divided into five sectors. A colonel with approximately five thousand soldiers was responsible for each sector. Each colonel's responsibilities included regaining the confidence of the population, helping to reestablish basic services, fighting insurgent forces, mentoring new Iraqi government leaders, and building a new Iraqi security force.

This time inclusion was accomplished by agreeing upon and monitoring a common set of metrics to measure progress toward these very complex objectives. These metrics provided the agenda for Dempsey's meetings with his colonels and the common vocabulary for their discussions. They knew that each of the multiple responsibilities had to be achieved and that progress would be most effective if they were achieved in parallel. The group met frequently to share best practices while also acknowledging that each sector provided its own particular challenges.

Inclusion was achieved across the 32,000 soldiers of the First Armored Division by establishing a common commitment to learning, listening, amplifying, and then adapting. The more complex the environment became, the more Dempsey encouraged individuals at every level to simply seek to positively influence it. In that way, everyone felt ownership—and inclusion—in a very important, very dynamic, and very unpredictable mission.

Whether leading forty-five, five thousand, or thirty thousand soldiers, the need to establish an environment of inclusion persisted. General Dempsey ended his career forty-one years after it had begun. In the last five years, he was a member of the Joint Chiefs of Staff, first as Chief of Staff of the Army and finally as the Chairman of the Joint Chiefs. He had started with forty-five soldiers and ended his career leading almost two million men and women of all the military services, active, guard, and reserve.

The scope and scale of the challenge had definitely changed, but the key to success had not. When the Joint Chiefs—Chairman, Vice Chairman, Army, Navy, Air Force, Marines, and National Guard—worked together, when they felt as though they were included in the decisions at the highest level of the Department of Defense, decisions were better: with greater ownership, their implementation was much more effective.

As Chairman, General Dempsey was also responsible for maintaining a peer-to-peer relationship with America's fifty-three allies and partners across the globe. America is blessed that it can and does dominate militarily when and where it chooses to do so. As a direct consequence of our dominant military power, we must demonstrate to our allies and partners that we value their contributions and understand their unique needs in our relationship. Stated another way, if we are to maintain our relationships, we need to embrace and manifest an instinct for inclusion. It simply can't be otherwise. The stronger partner in the relationship bears more of the responsibility for sustaining and enhancing the relationship. That is true in individual relationships, and it is true in the relationships among nation-states.

Following World War II, America made the deliberate decision to base our own national security on a carefully crafted system of alliances and partnerships. It has stood the test of time, kept us safe, and guaranteed a global order favorable to our interests. If that system is to be preserved, time, energy, and resources must continue to be invested in sustaining the inclusion necessary for it to be effective.

Today General Dempsey teaches leadership at Duke University. One of the leadership attributes he highlights in his discussions with students is "sense-making." That is, it is the responsibility of leaders at all levels to "make sense" of what's going on for their employees or, in the case of the military, for their junior leaders.

In forty-five years in uniform, General Dempsey experienced his fair share of both successes and failures. Generally, success came when everyone involved understood the task, the opportunities, and the limitations. Failures were the result of a lack of understanding, missed opportunity, and an inability to recognize limitations.

Inclusion unlocks understanding and opportunity. Inclusion is the elixir against uncertainty and misunderstanding. It's as simple as that.

We remind our readers that the principles and instincts that support the leadership theory described in this book are effective only when utilized as a set supporting one another. Each is necessary, but none is sufficient alone. We also remind our readers that the principles and instincts will always benefit from repetition, reemphasis, and reinforcement. Successful leaders will approach each day with the mind-set that every move and decision be made with the principles and instincts in mind.

We urge each of you as leaders to embrace inclusion as what is needed to move forward in the context of the changing world, and to pass this message along to your team members and fellow leaders. The importance of the message goes beyond one of successful leadership.

We believe that what pulls us apart today, whether in business, the military, or politics, is exclusion. Unless leaders pay attention to inclusion, they will begin to lose their competitive advantage. We must become more attuned to the issue of belonging, develop a bias for action, learn to relinquish control when we feel power slipping, and thus cultivate an environment of inclusiveness within our teams, organizations, communities, and countries.

As we face our problems, leaders must operate with the understanding that the more knowledge we harvest from all ends of our organizations, the more inclusion we generate. And the more inclusion we can build, the more likely we are to solve our problems. Even more so, the solutions to our problems are far more likely to endure when we support them with inclusion.

Inclusion should not be dismissed as just another "feel-good" movement, urging us to share power and control simply for the sake of being fair to one another; it has the power to change the world. Inclusion is what will give successful companies and countries an advantage as they work to grow and then sustain power in a hypercompetitive, information-supercharged environment. In this sense, inclusion is the way of the future.

CHAPTER 14: **RADICAL INCLUSION**

The general and the guru set out to write a leadership book, but they discovered something much more profound. They learned, amplified, and brought clarity to the reality that our sense of belonging has changed, that the more technology connects us, the further we grow apart and the more we highlight our differences and ignore our similarities. Under the influence of *digital echoes*, we are becoming more isolated, more suspicious, less positive, and less optimistic. This is affecting the way we interact with one another in government, in the workplace, domestically, and globally.

One hundred years ago, in the second decade of the twentieth century, the world went to war. In 1919, writing about the aftermath of World War I in Europe and about the Irish War of Independence with Great Britain, poet William Butler Yeats expressed the anxiety of the times in a poem he titled "The Second Coming." He used Christian imagery of the apocalypse and Second Coming allegorically to describe the collapse of innocence, of order, of restraint, of compassion, and ultimately of civilization. He mused about what would take its place:

The ceremony of innocence is drowned;
The best lack all conviction while the worst
Are full of passionate intensity . . .
. . . now I know that twenty centuries of sleep
were vexed to nightmare by a rocking cradle,
And what rough beast, its hour come round at last
Slouches toward Bethlehem to be born?

We wonder what poets will write of our time.

This is a book of leadership principles, but it also asserts that in the era of digital echoes, post-truth, rapid change, intense scrutiny, and supercharged emotion, well-meaning men and women, all of us, must think differently—radically—about inclusion.

Radical inclusion to counter inequities, intolerances, biases, and manipulations—the things that erode trust and render leadership ineffective.

Radical inclusion to promote integrity, empathy, collaboration, ownership, and accountability—the things that build trust and make leadership effective.

The general and the guru are indeed pragmatic. But we're also worried. History doesn't repeat, but it does rhyme.

CONCLUSION

For those who aspire to lead, the future is rich with opportunity. Issues will continue to become more complex, mutate more rapidly, and draw more scrutiny. Technology will provide more data and more accessibility. Leading will be exciting, and it will be dynamic.

Great leadership will be even more important than it is today, and it's obviously crucial today.

It will also be harder: harder in an environment that can produce paralyzing choices, ubiquitous distractions, and dramatic polarization; harder because of the corresponding increase in suspicion, disappointment, anger, and skepticism.

The things that allow people to become more informed and more connected, to organize their lives, to work from home, and to develop global social networks are the same things that allow them to choose what they want to know, to block out what they do not, to avoid personal contact, and to be recruited for causes good and bad.

We don't know how much more difficult leading will become, but we know—for sure—that it will become more difficult. We know—for sure—that it will take more of everything: more attention, more learning, more effort. And more inclusion.

It's been said that certain things are best seen with peripheral vision. The idea is that too much clarity, too much focus, and too much definition can obscure the richness, depth, and complexity of some subjects.

The things that make men and women effective leaders fall into that category.

• • •

In *Radical Inclusion* we have proffered several leadership principles and expressed our conviction about several leadership instincts. We suggest that the application of any one of them will improve a leader's relationship with his or her followers, but we concede that even adherence to all of them will not guarantee a leader's success.

On the other hand, we strongly believe that the environment we describe—including prominently the emergence of digital echoes—requires leaders to recognize, understand, and commit to inclusion as a leadership imperative.

Here's our bottom line. Inclusion is harder and can be slower, but it is a necessary precondition for achieving effective, efficient, and enduring solutions to complex problems.

Yes, inclusion can positively affect fairness and equality in the workplace, which yields greater trust between leader and follower. But more importantly, it's about persistent learning, shared ownership of decisions, and deeper commitment to the implementation of those decisions.

It's about developing trust by listening, amplifying, and including.

It's not a silver bullet, but it is an accelerator of the best ideas and a brake against the worst ideas.

Radical Inclusion acknowledges complexity and seeks to mitigate the risks inherent in the era of digital echoes. Failure to recognize and adapt to this new reality, failure to deeply embrace inclusion, would be the defining leadership failure of the twenty-first century.

ACKNOWLEDGMENTS

If we've learned anything from the experience of writing this book, it's that assembling a team of smart, confident, dedicated people of diverse backgrounds willing to challenge one another's thinking produces the best results. We deeply appreciate Tom Rath for his insights and experience; Piotr Juszkiewicz, our publisher, for his passion and drive; John Hutchinson for helping us discover the digital echo; Chip Colbert for helping us bridge the military and business worlds; Rachel Vick for her careful research and her patient management of two people who aren't easily managed; Sanyin Siang for her confidence in us and for helping us draw out our common insights about leadership; Mary Samson for her unfailing attention to detail; Ruth Schenkel for sharing her ideas about listening and amplifying voices; Hilary Roberts for her brilliance and clarity with our modest prose; and Paul Petters for his meticulous proofreading.